DISASTER OFF
MARTHA'S
VINEYARD

DISASTER OFF MARTHA'S VINEYARD

THE SINKING OF THE *CITY OF COLUMBUS*

THOMAS DRESSER

Charleston   London

THE
History
PRESS

Published by The History Press
Charleston, SC 29403
www.historypress.net

Front cover courtesy of James Claflin of LighthouseAntiques.net.

Back cover, top, courtesy of Eric Takakjian. Bottom, courtesy of Martha's Vineyard Museum.

First published 2012

Manufactured in the United States

ISBN 978.1.60949.510.7

Library of Congress Cataloging-in-Publication Data

Dresser, Tom.
Disaster off Martha's Vineyard : the sinking of the City of Columbus / Thomas Dresser.
p. cm.
Includes bibliographical references and index.
ISBN 978-1-60949-510-7
1. City of Columbus (Steamer) 2. Steamboat disasters--Massachusetts--Martha's Vineyard.
3. Shipwrecks--Massachusetts--Martha's Vineyard. I. Title.
G530.C52 2012
910.9163'46--dc23
2012009490

This book is dedicated to the young children who perished in this tragic shipwreck. Their memory shall be preserved.

I also dedicate this book to two new grandchildren, Jocelyn Sage Smyth and Henry Richard Held. May their lives be full and happy.

The following recipe appeared in the Vineyard Gazette *shortly after the shipwreck, on February 29, 1884:*

"A prize problem in navigation. Given: One Devil's bridge, one cold captain, one lookout who doesn't look out, a mate who does not comprehend an order, and a warm state room; mix three lighthouses, one steamship and one hundred twenty passengers; add a fresh gale and a supply of ignorance or stupidity, or both; sift out the intelligence supposed to exist in every pilot house, head for the nearest reef, and calculate the result."

Contents

CONTENTS

Forewords

There are limits to this kind of shipwreck book, or any disaster-specific book for that matter. Yes, shipwrecks are fascinating topics. Yes, they offer a unique window into the past. Yes, they sell. But few answer the "so what" question. Why, besides bearing witness, should we care about this or that particular wreck? Most shipwreck monographs are "insular" texts; or, to borrow a phrase from my dissertation advisor, they are "conversation enders" rather than "conversation starters." The former are important for populating the past with names, dates and facts, but they too often veer toward chronicle rather than history. Conversation starters, however, are the stuff of history—books that suggest new ways of conceiving the past; books that raise more questions than they answer; books that make an argument that grates against others' conceptions of the past.

Shipwrecks were everyday disasters along the coast during the nineteenth century. Few claimed as many lives as the *City of Columbus* tragedy, but every wreck altered, if only slightly, the social, cultural and economic landscape of industrializing America. What can these shipwrecks tell us about our past? How can they shed light on our understanding of the development of the coast or the role of disasters in history? For as thrilling as the stories of individual shipwreck are, it's the questions they raise rather than the answers they give that make shipwrecks truly fascinating conversation starters.

Jamin Wells
ShipsontheShore.com, 2011

From the time thousands of years ago when Wampanoag tribal members first traveled on it and continuing to today, Vineyard Sound has been a useful highway for vessels voyaging up and down the coast. However, because of currents, shoals and rocks, it is also a potentially dangerous passage, as the wrecks that lay beneath its waters starkly testify.

In the nineteenth century, before the Cape Cod Canal or major highways existed, it was the second-busiest waterway in the world behind the English Channel. In 1870, the Gay Head lighthouse keeper recorded that 26,469 vessels passed by his station bound either up or down the sound. Though dangerous, it was surrounded by the lighthouses, lightships and buoys that this volume of traffic required.

While there have been many wrecks around the sound, the *City of Columbus* is perhaps its most famous, most tragic and, in many ways, its most inexplicable. A contemporary account of the tragedy in *Harper's Weekly* called it "cruelly causeless." Even those of us accustomed to twenty-four-hour instant news outlets have to be impressed with how quickly the newspapers of the day covered the story and how widely it was reported, complete with dramatic illustrations of the wreck and the heroic efforts to rescue those on board.

The ship was relatively new, equipped with the latest equipment, commanded by an experienced master and sailed by an experienced crew on a familiar route, and the night was clear. What happened? Despite the fact that an official inquiry looked into the incident and rendered a judgment, questions about what was—or perhaps more importantly, was not—done that night and why have been the basis for countless discussions among mariners ever since that fateful night.

Those who go "down to the sea in ships" know that, even in seemingly tranquil conditions, the sea is always dangerous, and regardless of how new and well-equipped, the most critical component of any vessel and voyage is the crew—the human beings aboard and what they do or do not do. This lesson, in spite of GPS systems, autopilots and alarms, is still as true today as it was in 1884, as the recent wreck of a huge cruise ship, the *Costa Concordia*, off the coast of Italy dramatically demonstrates.

Thanks to Tom Dresser's careful research, we can return to 1884 and try to understand the "cruelly causeless" story that captivated the country.

Matthew Stackpole
Former Executive Director, Martha's Vineyard Museum
Historian, Charles W. Morgan Restoration Project, Mystic Seaport

Edouard Stackpole, Matthew's father, wrote the introduction to George A. Hough Jr.'s Disaster on Devil's Bridge *(1963) about the wreck of the* City of Columbus.

Acknowledgements

I credit three generations of the Hough family for inspiration and information in writing this book. George A. Hough Jr. (1894–1976) was the publisher of the *Falmouth Enterprise* and wrote *Disaster on Devil's Bridge* in 1963. (His brother, Henry Beetle Hough, edited the *Vineyard Gazette* for years.) George A. Hough Jr.'s work was thorough and thoughtful. I owe him a huge debt of gratitude for his efforts. My advantage, nearly a half century after his book was published, is that I have access to the Internet. Much of my research was conducted within the confines of the computer.

George III, son of George Jr., says, "My father was a good reporter, you know. I don't think there's a piece of information he didn't pursue in writing that book." Mr. Hough and his wife, Mary Lu, invited us to photograph an artifact his family had retrieved from the *City of Columbus*.

John Hough, George Jr.'s grandson and nephew of George III, suggested I write this updated version of the story of the *City of Columbus*. John has been a good friend and taught me a great deal in his (fiction) writing group. I try to apply his myriad writing techniques to my nonfiction efforts.

Any good work of nonfiction depends on solid research. I recognize the following people for their assistance in this project: Diane Parks, reference librarian at the Boston Public Library; Walter Hickey of the National Archives in Waltham; the staff of the Oak Bluffs and Vineyard Haven Libraries; Anna Carringer, Bonnie Stacy and Dana Street of the Martha's Vineyard Museum; Scott Price, United States Coast Guard historian; Erin Lopater at the Mariners Museum; Beth Nilsson of the Humane Society; and Irene Axelrod and Paula Richter at the Peabody Essex Museum.

Experts in the field were most helpful. Eric Takakjian detailed his successful efforts to discover the sunken ship. James Claflin provided background data on the Humane Society, lighthouses and artifacts associated with the shipwreck. Richard Boonisar offered photographs and information on the U.S. Life Saving Service and the wreck of the *City of Columbus*. And Jamin Wells has uncovered a wealth of shipwreck data, which he generously shared.

Personal interviews provided valuable information. My thanks to John Alley, Chris Baer, Arnie Carr, Todd Christy, Paul Cournoyer, George Dresser, Dick Goodell, Sam Low, June Manning, Mabelle Medowski, Casey Reagan, Jane Slater, Matthew Stackpole, Paul Sullivan, Anne Vanderhoop and Beverly Wright.

Through the Internet or snail mail, others offered assistance: Kathryn Balistrieri, Rick Bart, Lonnie Clark, Ron Crooker, Jim Jenney, Maureen Keillor, Roxy Leeson, Victor Mastone, Kim McKeithan, Chris Melrose, Rob Morris, Tom Mulloy, William Quinn, Cheryl Sloane and Evan Smith.

And I appreciate the encouragement and support of The History Press crew, from Jeff Saraceno to Jaime Muehl to Dani McGrath. You are worthy members of a worthy enterprise.

I would be remiss if I did not credit my wife, Joyce, for her steady hand on the wheel when the winds of words overwhelmed me or caustic calms frustrated my progress. She kept me on an even keel as I weathered the storms that challenged completion of this manuscript. Thanks Joyce!

Prologue

It is the deepest, darkest hour of the night. I am asleep in a strange berth, swaying gently to the rocking of the ship. I went to bed comfortably content after a sumptuous repast, prepared by professional chefs and served by elegantly attired waitstaff in our spacious dining saloon.

My demeanor is calm as I feel myself carried across the waters, heading south along the New England shores as people have done for years. It is an adventure, but not an unusual one. Scores of fellow passengers sleep peacefully in their staterooms nearby. Additional persons are bunked in the steerage berths, below on the main deck, forward.

I reflect on the comforts of this elegant vessel, with its inlaid panels, plush carpets, maroon cushions and embroidered chairs. I savor a sense of satisfaction, of accomplishment, of earned comfort. A feeling of contentment has dominated my sense of self since we left Boston yesterday afternoon.

The captain of the ship has nearly four decades of nautical experience and has navigated this route dozens of times. He has been a licensed pilot for fifteen years. The crew appears knowledgeable and courteous, practiced in handling both cargo and the whims of passengers.

The ship steams around Cape Cod, through Nantucket Sound and then enters Vineyard Sound. Ahead lie Block Island and the open sea, clear down the coast on this three-day trek to the comfortable clime of Savannah, Georgia, with its proximity to Florida's warmer weather. The desired destination presents an inviting refuge from the brutality of the frigid New England winter.

I sleep peacefully, rocking to the waves, aware, perhaps, of the brisk wind but calmed by the steady pulse of the twin propellers efficiently driving the steamship forward at a steady ten knots an hour. I wake briefly as my roommate stirs and then settles back to sleep. I drift off again. It is the deepest, darkest hour of the night.

A crunching sound comes from the forward part of the vessel. The hesitation only slightly disturbs my slumber. The ship pauses. I feel the vessel tilt slightly, stop a moment and then rock backward, awkwardly. I am waking up. Or is this a dream? I hear a shout, then another. The ship grinds to a halt. Panicked screams interrupt my consciousness. My world tilts to one side. As I rise from my berth, the floor seems to slide backward beneath my feet.

What is happening? What should I do? What about my roommate? This is unreal. It's the middle of the night. What is the matter? I'm still in my nightclothes. Is this a bad dream, a nightmare? The ship settles back on itself, toward the stern, and I realize something is wrong. Something is terribly wrong.

Shouts ring outside in the corridor. Someone knocks on my stateroom door. Now I am fully awake. I sense the ship shift again beneath my feet. I lose my grip on the door and wobble unsteadily by my bed. What should I do?

Gradually, it comes to me that I am in a crisis. Who is there to help me? I search about for clothes, a life preserver, a companion or a crew member to direct me. I tug open my door and face chaos in the corridor. People stampede from their rooms toward the companionway, up to the top deck. It is dark. It is crowded. The engines are now quiet, but the wind whistles as I make my way up the stairs, unsure what awaits.

As I reach the top of the ship, the hurricane deck, crisis grips everyone around me. Screams and shouts permeate the darkness, chaotic and desperate. Some of the crew slash lines to free the lifeboats. Women clutch their children, their husbands. No one knows what to do.

The wind blows with greater intensity. The ship lists or leans to the left, to port, lurching passengers about as the deck becomes unsteady. Waves break over the side as the ship squats broadside to the wind, now even more fierce. Passengers crowd up the companionway behind me, pushing me forward, seeking salvation.

I am frightened. Surrounded by people in a state of panic, I feel I have lost control of my own life. I was roused from a peaceful slumber to face this most devastating disaster. And no one can tell me what to do.

Lifeboats are lowered haphazardly from their davits but crash helplessly against the heeling hull of the ship or capsize when they hit the water. A life raft washes overboard, spilling its passengers into the seas. A woman's lifeless body, still in her nightclothes, floats by my feet.

The fear on people's faces frightens me. Nothing at hand can protect me. Women and children are washed off the deck of the ship and into the sea. No one helps them. The older gentleman who sat with me at dinner is carried over the rails. No one can prevent the seas from causing more death and destruction. There is no hope. A small child is swept from his mother's arms.

A crew member grasps at the stays or lines in the rigging and hoists himself aloft. The captain crawls atop the pilothouse, the highest structure of the sinking ship. More men pull themselves above the devastation of the waves, the carnage of the seas, the death ship. Still more passengers emerge from the steerage compartment, deep in the recesses of the ship. They crowd up and out the stairways as the stern of the ship quivers and sinks beneath the waves. The only salvation is in the rigging, but I do not have the wherewithal to hoist myself aloft.

The wind whistles menacingly. Waves continue to lash loose lines. A seaman dangling from the shrouds falls into the threatening ocean. Another wave washes a woman off the ship's sloping, slanting deck. I see a young seaman climb higher in the rigging as a mother and her infant are washed overboard.

It is the deepest, darkest hour of the night.

1
The Wreck

Eric Takakjian of Fairhaven has had an addiction since his early teens. It shows no signs of abating and has had a definite impact on his life. He feeds his habit by working as a tugboat captain and proprietor of Quest Marine Services.

Eric dives. He spends his free time and any extra funds to dive for shipwrecks. He took his first dive when he was twelve years old and has conducted more than five thousand dives in the past forty years. This is a serious habit, one he thrives on, obsesses over and continues to perfect.

One wreck in particular intrigued Eric. He was curious about the location of the *City of Columbus*, which was off course and went down by Gay Head, now Aquinnah, off Martha's Vineyard in the winter of 1884. He had heard rumors that the ship was broken up and salvaged by wreckers in the late 1800s. Other stories indicated that the wreck was buried beneath the tons of sand that wash around Gay Head. He set his mind on discovering if any remains of the vessel were still extant more than a century after it foundered beneath the beam of the Gay Head lighthouse.

For years, Eric poured over photographs, charts and accounts, both personal and public, of the disaster. He focused on one image, a photograph taken the day after the ship sank. In that picture, the bow of the *City of Columbus* is still partially above water, aligned with the cliffs of Gay Head. Eric thought he could determine the exact location of the wreck based on triangulation between the mast of the ship, the distance from and the height of the cliffs and the depth of the ship below water. If the *City of Columbus* were still there, Eric would find it.

This photograph, taken one day after the shipwreck, was instrumental in finding the location of the sunken vessel. Triangulation between the depth of the ship in the water and its relation to the cliffs solved the equation. *In the collection of Richard Boonisar, an authority on the U.S. Life Saving Service and the Humane Society, photograph by Thomas Dresser.*

When he lined up the top of the foremast against the cliffs, he determined the ship had struck the uppermost ledge of Devil's Bridge, a submerged boulder nearly a half mile off shore. And it struck from the north. As he gauged how much of the main deck was still above water in the photograph, he could ascertain the present water depth where the vessel lay. Using these two calculations, the distance from the cliffs and the depth of the water, Eric plotted a point on navigational charts that indicated the potential location of the wreck, assuming it sank at the Devil's Bridge boulder and did not drift far.

Eric is part of an active group of fellow divers, equally as intrigued by the deep as he. Other members of the dive team who searched for the *City of Columbus* in the spring of 2000 included his wife Lori, Dave and Pat Morton, Tom Mulloy, Tom and Kathy Murray, Steve Scheuer, Dennis Sevene and Charlie Warzecha. In diving, Eric is very clear that it is a team effort; there is no room for egos. It is a "we" undertaking.

On a late spring day in June 2000, they set off. Eric calculated the wreck would be between .59 and .69 mile off the southern tip of Gay Head, beyond the lighthouse. He motored over the site initially, to get a visual impression of the waters, and then located the optimum point to anchor. He and a fellow diver, Charlie Warzecha, went down.

Each diver had a reel line that he attached to the boat's anchor line. This served two purposes: it would bring them back, and it would keep them in touch with each other.

From a diver's perspective, they did not have to dive very deep to find the ship. The ocean floor, at this point, is less than fifty feet below the surface. For experienced divers, this is easy, as they need not worry about narcosis, loss of nitrogen in their body due to water pressure. They omit the decompression stage, a time-consuming wait required when emerging from waters over one hundred feet. The *City of Columbus* experience borders on recreational diving for these experts, except they were unsure what they would find.

In Eric's account of the experience, documented in his Quest Marine Services report, he writes, "The dive plan was for both divers to proceed to the end of the anchor line and clip off their wreck reels." Eric swam to the right, and Charlie dove to the left, and within twenty feet Charlie "ended up swimming into the starboard bow of the *City of Columbus*! Research had paid off big time."

The other members of the team followed Eric and Charlie into the deep and explored the wreck. They were the first exploratory team to locate the *City of Columbus* and determine the extent of destruction since 1884. Their dive was an important step in the chronicle of this shipwreck.

Examination of the wreck indicated the ship lies on the sandy bottom of the north ledge of the Devil's Bridge. The lower portions of the ship's hull are buried in sand. The stern rests about fifty feet below the surface; the bow is higher, about thirty-five feet below. The ship faces west. Massive boulders surround the wreck, and much of the ship is, indeed, buried in sand. Eric notes that "portions of hull plating and framing are exposed in some places, particularly in the stern." They found the ship's compound engine, line shaft bearings and hull sheathing around the wreck. Parts of the wreck, however, had been salvaged.

The decks and superstructure, or outer surfaces, of the *City of Columbus*, made of wood, have rotted away or been broken apart by the force of the water. Debris from the ship lies nearby. Because the *City of Columbus* is not on the approved list of Massachusetts exempt shipwrecks, amateur and professional divers and salvage operators are forbidden to remove artifacts from the wreck.[1]

Eric and his team have been back to the *City of Columbus*. Many times. So many times that Eric cannot quote a specific number of dives, but it's more than twenty. He says the white sand and rock on the bottom provide excellent visibility, and the wreck sits between thirty and fifty feet below the

Underwater images of the sunken ship in the waters of Devil's Bridge off Gay Head: *top*, engine foundations and frame, with diver; *bottom*, frames and hull plating aft on the starboard side. *Photographs by Tom Mulloy and Eric Takakjian.*

surface. He cautions, "In exploring the wreck over the past few years we have found that parts of the site will cover and uncover as the sand is displaced or filled in, due primarily to the wave action of winter storms." He notes that the tidal current may run as high as three knots, which means recreational divers should dive in slack water, with no tidal movement. Winter diving can improve underwater visibility as there is little algae to interfere with visibility.

The *City of Columbus* sank shortly after it ran onto Devil's Bridge on January 18, 1884. Eric Takakjian located the wreck on June 11, 2000. Now, amateur divers can explore the wreck, swimming among the bass, fluke and scup that have had the ship to themselves for the past 128 years. As Eric says of finding the wreck of the *City of Columbus*, "It closed a chapter in New England maritime history."

The Ship

The city of Columbus, Georgia, was named for the explorer Christopher Columbus. Settlers chose a site high on a bluff overlooking the Chattahoochee River at its most northern navigable point. The city sits on a natural plateau between north Georgia's Piedmont region at the foot of the Blue Ridge Mountains and the southern coastal plains.

Today, with a population of 190,000, Columbus is the third-largest city in Georgia and has the largest incorporated area. The city is situated on the state line between Georgia and Alabama, south of Atlanta; east of Montgomery, Alabama; and southeast of Birmingham, Alabama. Columbus is 250 miles west of Savannah, and Macon is 100 miles away. The army's Fort Benning is southeast of the city.

Although quite warm in the summer, Columbus boasts a mean temperature of sixty degrees and a growing season for two-thirds of the year. Recreational activities provide a popular draw for the area, with waterfalls, nearby mountains and the beauty of the plains all in a temperate zone.

Columbus was established as a frontier town in western Georgia in 1828 near the site of a Native American settlement. It developed as a profitable trade nexus. Situated on the Chattahoochee River, Columbus abutted the Federal Road, and the railroad connected it to the North. A shipping industry evolved with the success of the textile trade, which transported manufactured cotton products south to New Orleans and beyond.

At the onset of the Civil War in 1861, Columbus was considered a key industrial hub of the South, supplying uniforms and weaponry to the Confederacy. At the end of the war, just a few days after Lee surrendered and Lincoln was assassinated, on Easter Sunday, April 16, 1865, troops on both sides, unaware that the war was over, fought the Battle of Columbus. Union forces burned the city.

By the late 1870s, Columbus had been rebuilt. The city thrived on the rebirth of the textile industry. A popular periodical of the era, *Frank Leslie's Illustrated News*, reported on local textile production: "Fancy colored goods, and embrace cheviots, ginghams, tickings, plaids and kindred styles." Of the influx of manufacturing, it noted, "These mills add about 8,000 to the population of the city, and make them happy and contented." The paper added, "All this has been built since 1865, and with Southern money."

Columbus was a prosperous Georgia city in the 1870s. Naming a ship for the city recognized the prominence of this western metropolis as a symbol of the rebounding South in the era of Reconstruction. Thus, it was appropriate for the Ocean Steamship Company to name one of its newly commissioned ships after this bustling metropolis. The steamship *City of Columbus* was a well-appointed vessel, designed to transport both cargo and passengers to and from Savannah.

The evolution of the steamship in the nineteenth century set a precedent for American transportation. The first steamboat was designed by John Fitch; he steamed by Philadelphia's Constitutional Convention on the Delaware River in 1787. Two decades later, in 1807, Robert Fulton powered his *Clermont* up the Hudson River from New York to Albany. Eighty years later, the Ocean Steamship Company was only one of several businesses that provided transport along the coast. Steamships proved more efficient and reliable than sail and were faster than the locomotive.

John Roach and Son, of Chester, Pennsylvania, built the ship from hull to engine. Roach, an Irish immigrant, founded the Delaware River Iron Ship Building and Engine Works Company, which became the predominant shipbuilder of the late 1870s.

The *City of Columbus* was built in 1878. It was initially launched in the Delaware River, near Philadelphia, and sailed to New York and thence to Savannah. That event was duly reported by numerous local and national newspapers: "The new iron steamship *City of Columbus* was successfully launched from John Roach & Son ship yard this afternoon, in the presence of a large concourse of people. She is 272 feet long, 38 feet 6 inches beam; depth of hold, 24 feet 10 inches, and has a tonnage of 2250 tons. She is for the Ocean Steamship Company, of Savannah, Ga., and will ply between that city and New York."[2] (The actual dimensions of the *City of Columbus* were 275 feet long and 38 feet wide; the largest steamship that plies Vineyard

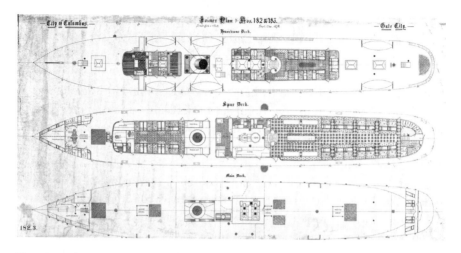

Plans for the *City of Columbus* provide a detailed description of the vessel. It was 275 feet long, 20 feet longer than the steamship *Island Home*. The top deck was the hurricane, the middle was the spar and the lowest was the main. *Courtesy of the Mariner's Museum, Newport News, Virginia.*

Sound between Martha's Vineyard and Wood's Hole is the *Island Home*, which is 255 feet long and 64 feet wide, so the *City of Columbus* was longer and narrower than the *Island Home*.)

The *City of Columbus* was described as a vessel that "possessed the highest rating possible, with an A-1 classification and was amply provided with fixtures, life preservers and boats as required by law."[3] It carried six metallic lifeboats, with a keg of water and tins of biscuits in each. "On every trip it was customary to hold a thorough boat drill," one newspaper noted.[4]

Great excitement was generated by reports of this newest vessel in the Ocean Steamship Company line. "The *City of Columbus* is an addition to the fleet of the Ocean Steamship Line, of Savannah and recently sailed on her first trip from this port."[5] In glowing prose, its singular accommodations were praised: "The main saloon is commodious, and, like the other new steamships of this line, is superbly finished in hard polished woods." No luxury was too extravagant. Other steamships on the line were the *City of Macon*, the *City of Savannah* and the *Gate City*.

The magazine *Scientific American* reported that the *City of Columbus* had three decks, with the top deck constructed of iron and covered with wooden flooring. The ship's hull was encased in iron sheathing, with seventh-eighths-inch-thick plating.

The power of the ship was described in detail, with its four boilers of a circular tubular type. Each boiler had three furnaces made of half-inch-thick iron. The furnaces burned coal, with pressure reaching eighty pounds per square inch, producing 1,500 horsepower. Twin propellers revolved once a second, on average, which resulted in a projected speed of twelve and a half knots per hour. That speed would vary depending on tide and wind, as well as cargo.

The three decks were the main, the spar and the hurricane. The main deck, the lowest, housed steerage passengers forward, an icehouse and the engine. The middle or spar deck was home to staterooms one through fourteen, the porter, the butcher, the pantry, the storeroom and the steering engine mechanism. There were more staterooms forward, labeled A through K. Two saloons, as well as a ladies' boudoir, were on this deck. The main saloon was one hundred feet long and served as a splendid dining area; expansive tables had cushioned couches on one side, against the wall, with revolving chairs on the opposite side. It was an imposing setting. A second, forward saloon offered additional space for passengers to gather.

The top deck was the hurricane deck. The pilothouse was forward, with a window that connected the adjoining captain's room and then the officers' rooms. Staterooms fifteen through thirty-two surrounded the Social Hall,

In the foreword to his book *Disaster on Devil's Bridge*, George A. Hough Jr. wrote of his neighbor's house: "Over the doorway to the seldom used parlor was an oval tablet of porcelain. It was fancily lettered in faded rose and black 'Social Hall.'" The plaque is now in the home of John and Kate Hough. *Photograph by Joyce Dresser.*

This door, perhaps from one of the ship's staterooms, bears a veneer of rosewood and walnut. *Courtesy of Martha's Vineyard Museum; photograph by Joyce Dresser.*

which dominated this deck. A grand staircase led from the Social Hall down to the main saloon on the spar deck. A great kerosene chandelier illuminated this area. Including the steerage berths and the forty-two staterooms, the *City of Columbus* could accommodate as many as two hundred passengers.

Some called it a floating palace:

> *There was, indeed, elegance in the saloons finished with exotic French walnut, mahogany, rosewood and birdseye maple. There was richness in the patterned softness of the axminister carpets (elegant British fabric). It was luxurious to sink into the overstuffed chairs and sofa upholstered in crimson plush. The grand stairway between lower and upper saloons was imposing in its wide sweep and elaborate balustrade. To the newspapers of*

the day it was a "novel and rare beauty." A large mirror at its top and the lamp suspended above added their touches of ornateness.[6]

The *City of Columbus* was fitted with elegant appointments, appropriate for the wealthy clientele enticed aboard. The steamship was deemed a safe, luxurious and reliable form of transport from the wintry weather of New England to the warmth of the South.

Below decks was additional space for cargo, which ranged from bales of cotton shipped north to manufactured goods and agricultural products headed south. The *City of Columbus* meant all things to all people, offering a commercial opportunity for businesses in both the North and South.

A second launch, more a promotional event than a functional floating, took place in Savannah, Georgia, in September 1878. The *Georgia Weekly Telegraph* announced that four hundred invitations had been sent to "prominent citizens of Columbus," suggesting they journey 250 miles, over twelve hours, by train to Savannah so they could "enjoy the pleasure of an excursion to the salts on the new and beautiful steamer." The invitation announced that aboard ship, guests would be party to "a grand ovation, a presentation of a handsome suit of colors and speeches and a general conviviality." The Ocean Steamship Company promoted its newest acquisition with an all-day recreational sail.

On the day of the excursion, the *Telegraph* reported that Columbus guests who traveled to Savannah would witness "the new steamship which 'walks

Chromolithograph of the *City of Columbus* under sail. The ship was launched in 1878 by the Ocean Steamship Company and sold to the Boston and Savannah Steamship Company in 1882. *Courtesy of Martha's Vineyard Museum; photograph by Joyce Dresser.*

the water' as the proud and beautiful representative of their city." The piece concluded, "The *City of Columbus* will take the party out on a sea excursion on Monday and no doubt they will have a very enjoyable time."

A third launch was announced, four years later, when the ship was purchased by Nickerson & Company, creating the Boston link in the coastal steamship chain:

> *The steamer* City of Columbus, *recently purchased by Nickerson & Co., arrived here yesterday from New York, under the command of Captain Wright. She has been running between New York and Savannah, but now takes her place on the Boston and Savannah line of packets. She is a screw steamer of 2,200 tons burthen, 300 feet long. She was built by John Roach & Son in 1878, and is a very serviceable boat.*[7]

Boston eagerly anticipated this new steamship and the formation of a new company, the Boston and Savannah Steamship Company.

By the time the *City of Columbus* became part of the Nickerson fleet in 1882, the ship was four years old and had admirably plied the waters between New York and Savannah.

3

The Route

Cotton connected Boston and Savannah. Prior to the Civil War, sailing ships transported cotton north to New England mills, where it was spun into thread and woven into cloth. Following the war, steamers were utilized to carry cotton. In 1869, F.W. Nickerson of Boston expanded his business with iron screw steamers, which made weekly trips transporting cotton north from September to April.

It was noted in the Boston press that the Boston and Savannah Steamship Company had been established with two steamers, the *City of Columbus* and the *Gate City*, with the intent of meeting the needs of both the South and the North.[8] Each ship could transport up to 4,400 bales of cotton.

To utilize the return trip headed south, the Steamship Company shipped fish and bacon, and "immense quantities of potatoes and apples are also taken out." In addition, "great numbers of pianos, organs, carriages, etc. are also taken out by these steamers." Clearly, steamships proved an efficient means of cargo transfer. And the voyage by sail was accomplished in three days, half the time of a trip by train.

In addition to cotton, turpentine was brought north. And "lumber, once brought in sailing vessels by slow and laborious process, may now be telegraphed for at the mills in Georgia, and fine yellow pine cargoes be landed in Boston within six days thereafter." Transportation expanded. "Immense quantities of early vegetables are thus shipped in excellent condition to Boston." With melons and oranges reaching New England, economic opportunity flourished. The newspaper concluded, "And thus these two sections, North and South, minister to the wants of each other."

The conventional route south from Boston was around Cape Cod, past Monomoy Point, through Nantucket Sound into Vineyard Sound and then past the Gay Head light on Martha's Vineyard. This route had been traversed by vessels large and small for decades. The *City of Columbus* took three days, or seventy-two hours, to make the run from Boston to Savannah.

Key lighthouses had been constructed strategically along the route to assist in nocturnal or stormy navigation. From West Chop (1817), Nobska (1829) and Tarpaulin Cove (1817) to Cuttyhunk (1823) and Gay Head (1799), lighthouses guarded the dangerous shores along Vineyard Sound. Buoys marked outcropping rocks or shallow reefs. The Sow and Pigs lightship (1847) was tethered off Cuttyhunk. (In November 1883, its anchor chain required repair, and the lightship was temporarily moored in Tarpaulin Cove. While there, it tangled with a schooner, "doing much damage to both." The lightship, known as *LV 41*, returned to service on February 2, 1884, two weeks after the wreck of the *City of Columbus*, so it was not actually in place at the time of the shipwreck.)

This first-order Fresnel lens, with over one thousand prisms, was installed in the Gay Head lighthouse in 1856. It flashed every ten seconds, with the fourth flash red instead of white. "I thought the light on Gay Head appeared a little closer than usual but did not attach much importance to the fact," explained Roderick McDonald, the man at the wheel. The Fresnel light is housed outside the Martha's Vineyard Museum, in Edgartown, Massachusetts. *Photograph by Joyce Dresser.*

The Sinking of the *City of Columbus*

With his many years of navigational experience, Captain Schuyler Wright, of the *City of Columbus*, was familiar with the lighthouses constructed along Vineyard Sound. And he certainly was cognizant of the quirky tidal flow of the area.

A cartographer by trade, George Eldridge of Chatham first published a book on the Monomoy Point Shoals, off the southeast "elbow" of Cape Cod, in 1854. That booklet contained information on the location of rocks and ledges to avoid when traversing the sound, but more was needed.

The flow of the tide in and out of Vineyard Sound is tricky. While it seems logical that the tide would flow in to the east and out to the west, in Vineyard Sound the tide gushes around Gay Head going north during the first hour or two when it floods (rises) and southerly in the first hour or two when it ebbs (falls). Thereafter, the tide flows east and west.

Eldridge's son, Captain George W. Eldridge of Martha's Vineyard, recognized the need and developed a tide book for the region. He first published his *Tide and Pilot Book* in 1875.[9]

Navigation may be thwarted or distorted by underwater barriers that have an impact on tidal flow. Chris Melrose studies oceanography and offers his thoughts on Vineyard Sound:

> *The shoals in Vineyard and Nantucket Sounds complicate the flow in the region by focusing currents in various spots. The shoals tend to move and change due to the action of the currents, like drifting dunes in the desert, and this makes charts of these shoals unreliable. Most of the Sound is pretty sandy, however, Devil's Bridge where the* City of Columbus *ran aground, is a shallow rock-studded spit sticking out from the tip of Gay Head that was particularly hazardous to ships.*

Melrose discussed the role of currents in tidal flow: "As for the currents, Vineyard Sound is sort of like a funnel that focuses tidal flow, producing strong currents that follow the tidal cycle and reverse about every six hours. Around where the *City of Columbus* sank, the current can exceed two knots." The speed of the tide, as well as its direction, must be considered when navigating the sound.

Flood tide at Pollock Rip Channel originates four hours after Boston's high tide. The current flows from the east when it floods and ebbs from the west. Water flows into Nantucket Sound at 0.8 miles per hour. In Vineyard Sound, it floods to the northeast and ebbs to the southwest at 1.4 miles per hour. A faster tide occurs along the Elizabeth Islands, on the northwest side of Vineyard Sound, where tidal speed can reach 2.6 miles per hour, swifter than in the middle of the sound. These anomalies are key to navigating the sound.

In Vineyard Sound, the tide ebbs at 0.6 miles per hour. Along the east coast of the Vineyard, it moves at 1.3 miles per hour, twice the speed, back up to Pollock Rip Channel, south of the elbow of Cape Cod. Slack tide is when there is no tidal movement—dead water, the pause between the ebb and flow.

High water at Gay Head registers nearly three feet above dead low tide. (The average tidal rise is 2.9 feet.) The average velocity of tidal flow in Vineyard Sound, both ebb and flood, is two knots.

Longtime sailor Paul Sullivan notes the impact of wind and tide:

> *The tide and winds play a very important part in navigating around the Vineyard. The wind always plays an important role, but the tides and current are also critical; you must know about them. The fact that the captain of the* City of Columbus *did not pay attention to the wind, the tides (if it had been high tide, they might have been okay, hard to speculate) and the currents would be the main reason they crashed, not so much whether it was day or night.*

Wind and tide are critical in navigation.

When the tide runs around the peninsula of Gay Head, it flows directly into the channel used by ships and thus affects their course. Eldridge warned, in his tide book, "Vessels bound into Vineyard Sound from the Westward, will have the current of ebb on the starboard bow." One would think the tide runs into Vineyard Sound from the east, but it actually flows north around Gay Head and into the channel, at least during the first two hours. With a strong wind blowing across open water (or fetch) from the west and an ebb tide flowing out through Vineyard Sound south and east, the combination of wind and tide would push a vessel closer to the Vineyard shores.

Another experienced sailor, Dick Goodell, explains, "The general direction of ebb and flood tide is southwest to northeast. Around Gay Head, the first two hours of flood and ebb tide, the direction of flood is due north and of ebb is due south. In both cases the tide pushes a ship closer to the Vineyard."

The Sinking of the *City of Columbus*

The rocky underwater ledge of Devil's Bridge is part of the Vineyard's glacial terminal moraine. The *City of Columbus* sheered off the top of an underwater boulder, the Devil's Back, causing the ship to sink. *Postcard courtesy of Judy and Peter Case.*

The first part of the flood tide runs nearly north and then gradually shifts east, farther into the sound.

When navigating these waters, use of dead reckoning determines the course. As Goodell says, "Part of dead reckoning considers the compass, the stars, the wind speed and direction, the current, the water depth, and ship speed. And if you don't know some of it, you can put yourself on the rocks."

Captain Eldridge promoted his book even as he warned sailors of the vicissitudes of sailing through the sound. "If you are bound into Vineyard Sound in thick weather, you will probably refer to the Gay Head and Cross Rip tables in this book, to see when the tide turns in or out."

The *Tide and Pilot Book* warns of unusual currents in Vineyard Sound. These currents create a turbulent area by the Elizabeth Islands, known as "the Graveyard." The Graveyard extends from Tarpaulin Cove on Naushon Island south to Sow and Pigs lightship off Cuttyhunk. The Graveyard is where ships foundered on the north side of Vineyard Sound, often due to the tidal speed of more than 2.5 miles per hour.

Eldridge asked, "Did it ever occur to you that seldom does a vessel go ashore on Gay Head or on the south side of the Sound? But that hundreds of them have been piled up in The Graveyard." Eldridge reported on dozens of ships wrecked along the shores due to rapid tidal flow. Besides the loss of his ship, "many a captain has lost his reputation there also." Captain Eldridge warned of potential disaster: "I have explained this matter, and I leave the rest to your judgment and careful consideration to keep your vessel out of the Graveyard."

The Cunard Line's 963-foot-long *Queen Elizabeth II*, more than three times the length of the *City of Columbus*, ran aground south of Cuttyhunk in August 1992, just beyond Eldridge's Graveyard. More than 2,500 passengers and crew had to be evacuated after the luxury liner sprang a hole in its hull when it scraped an uncharted underwater shoal.

Although navigational charts deemed the water deep enough for the vessel, the *Queen Elizabeth II* was moving so fast that it created a "squat effect," which means it actually drew more than its thirty-two-foot draft. This virtual vacancy in the water meant the ship rode lower at higher speeds; it was capable of steaming along at more than thirty miles per hour. While there were no injuries, and the ship continued on its route to New York for repairs, it exemplifies the hazards of navigation in the present day.

The *City of Columbus* safely skirted the Graveyard only to run aground just off Gay Head.

Chris Melrose adds to his assessment of the nautical travails along Vineyard Sound:

> *Before modern navigation aids like GPS and radar, crews needed to be able to see the stars or navigational references to know their position. Ships often found themselves blind in a storm with nothing but dead reckoning since their last fix to guess their position. You can imagine using dead reckoning in an area with strong and complex currents is difficult, particularly with more primitive propulsion systems or in bad weather.*

We have to assume that dead reckoning played a critical role in the disaster of the *City of Columbus*.

Captain Schuyler Wright assumed command of the *City of Columbus* in September 1882. Born in 1831 in Wareham, Massachusetts, Wright had been aboard ships since the age of thirteen. He knew the vicissitudes of the ocean, losing both his father and brother in nautical mishaps. Wright earned his pilot's license in 1869 at the age of thirty-seven. Now fifty-two, Captain Wright was at the pinnacle of his career.

Captain Wright was quite familiar with the route through Vineyard Sound. For decades he had navigated the sound; for sixteen months he had captained the *City of Columbus*. He knew the influence of the tides, the impact of the wind and variables such as speed of the ship, weight of the vessel and when to adjust the course. One more aspect of navigation was visibility.

A key component of nocturnal navigation was natural light. Sunset on January 17 occurred at 4:41 p.m., while the *City of Columbus* was steaming along the eastern shore of Cape Cod. The end of civil twilight was 5:11 p.m. (Civil twilight is the time frame, generally a half hour prior to sunrise or after sunset, when there is sufficient light to illuminate objects.)

Moonrise that night, at longitude 70.8 degrees west, latitude 41.3 degrees north, was at 10:23 p.m., so by the time the ship was on the rocks, at 3:30 a.m., the moon was high in the sky. The moon was in the waning gibbous phase; that is, the stage following a full moon when it had not yet reached the last quarter but was still more than half full. On that date, 73 percent of the visible disk of the moon was illuminated. The moon set at 10:10 a.m. on January 18 as the first rescue boats reached the wreck.

The impact of the moon on the tide was minimal. A spring tide floods with a full or new moon; a neap or smaller tide occurs with a half moon. On January 18, the moon was between full and half, so it would have had little effect on the strength of the tide.

Thus, the navigational tools for Captain Wright of the *City of Columbus* were in place, from lighthouses along the shore to the tide book to his years of nautical expertise and experience. He had navigated the ship through Vineyard Sound dozens of times.

But something went horribly wrong.

4
The Omens

The steamship City of Columbus, *from Boston, arrived at Savannah Georgia yesterday, having on board the captain and crew of the bark* Arthur C. Wade *which vessel the steamer ran into and sunk off Nantucket in a fog on Thursday night. The bark was loaded with sugar from Caibarien (a Cuban seaport) for Boston.*[10]

This news report was brief but portentous.

Two days later, there were more details:

There was a heavy fog prevailing at the time, and although the fog whistles and bells had been sounded, yet the discovery of the close proximity of each vessel to the other was not known until it was beyond the possibility of either to avert the danger. The City of Columbus, *after vainly endeavoring to back and impede her progress, which was of necessity, on account of the fog, very slow, struck the* Alice C. Waite [sic] *abaft midship on the port side.*[11]

The *Arthur C. Wade* sank within fifteen minutes.

Other than erring on the name of the sunken ship, this story corroborated the facts: the *City of Columbus* rammed and sank a sailing ship off the Nantucket shoals, in the fog, in the late morning of September 14, 1883. This was four months before the *City of Columbus* itself sank. According to press reports, the captain and crew "lost everything they possessed."

The barkentine *Arthur C. Wade* sailed out of Caibarien, Cuba, with a shipload of sugar on August 29, two weeks before the accident. When the

City of Columbus slammed into the sailing ship, Captain Wright steamed alongside and rescued the captain, his crew of ten and one young passenger. The barkentine sank quickly. The *City of Columbus*, undamaged, then steamed southward on its scheduled route with the rescued crew aboard. As the newspaper explained, "In the meantime, they are cared for and made to feel as happy and comfortable as is possible under the circumstances. They were all landed at the Savannah quarantine station."

This accident was revisited in a court case, settled more than a year later, on December 1, 1884. The freight of sugar aboard the *Wade* was estimated to be worth $2909.12, with an additional eight bales of tobacco worth $158.21. The ship itself was assessed at $22,350.00.

The incident occurred just south of Cape Cod in a thick, dense fog bank off the south shoal lightship between Nantucket and Monomoy Point. The *City of Columbus* was fully equipped with appropriate steam whistles, "as required by law," and a competent complement of crew was aboard. The steamer was "moving at a moderate, proper and lawful rate of speed, and every possible precaution were taken to avoid collision." Still, with the steamer progressing on its course of southwest by west, "the barkentine was seen indistinctly through the fog, just ahead and under the bows of the steamer and so near that a collision was inevitable, notwithstanding all possible efforts on the part of the steamer to avoid it."

Court testimony was concise: "The steamer struck the barkentine a blow—glancing aft on her port side, between the main and mizzen rigging, and the barkentine soon afterwards sank."

One other angle that may or may not relate to this incident is that Captain Wright of the *City of Columbus* had to reprimand his second mate, Augustus (Gus) Harding. In the official inquiry of the wreck of the *City of Columbus* in February 1884, it was noted that an incident was reported "some five months ago, when Harding varied the ship's course a little. He [Wright] corrected him and told him never to do it again."

Apparently, there was a second incident in which Harding was reprimanded by Captain Wright for veering off course; this, too, surfaced during the investigation of the sinking of the *City of Columbus*. And Gus Harding was on duty, the man in charge of the ship, at the time of the wreck at Gay Head.

One may draw one's own conclusions.

After a disaster, we often hear stories of people who had predicted it. Of course, there are ominous feelings when nothing happens, but in the case of the *City of Columbus*, three accounts come down to us from people who feared disaster would strike the steamer. And in two instances, fate played a role.

Nathaniel Morton was a rising star in the field of journalism in the 1880s. He worked first for the *Taunton Gazette* and then the *New Bedford Mercury* and was promoted to the *Boston Globe* in 1880. Early in 1884, Morton acted on his physician's advice to travel south for his health; consumption wracked his lungs. He planned to take a steamer.

When Morton booked his reservation on the *Gate City*, he was assigned a stateroom with a stranger. Rather than have to share his room, he opted to

This Bible from the vessel is stored in an Amazon.com box in the vault of the Chilmark Town Hall. Mrs. Nahum T. Norton, the former Abbie O. Rotch, salvaged the Bible on the north shore of Chilmark, near the Paint Mill. The Bible advertises that it was "translated from the original tongues," with 100,000 marginal references and included Dr. William Smith's Standard Bible Dictionary. It was inscribed as a gift to Loisa Hartruber from her loving husband, Gerhard, on September 6, 1883. *Courtesy of Todd Christie; photograph by Joyce Dresser.*

The Sinking of the *City of Columbus*

The *City of Columbus* at Nickerson's Wharf in Boston. The ship's hold was twenty-four feet deep and could handle 2,250 tons. With twin propellers on a coal-fired steam engine, the ship moved along at twelve knots. *Courtesy of Eric Takakjian/Quest Marine Services, Peabody Essex Museum and the Mariner's Museum, Newport News, Virginia.*

take the next steamer. The *City of Columbus* sailed the following fortnight, and Nathaniel Morton had a stateroom to himself.

During meal service, Morton requested "a warm place at the table," according to Pitman, the chief steward, "as his lungs were not strong." When the ship went down, he never made it out on deck.

At the last minute, just before the steamer left port, three men from Lawrence—James Brown, Sampson Fawcett and James Walker—bought steerage tickets at fifteen dollars each. Only Brown survived. Again, fate seemed to play a role in their last-minute decision.

Mr. James Beal, of Mattapan, had traveled to Florida three months before his wife and eighteen-year-old daughter. He had already suffered the loss of three children, and now he claimed a premonition of the shipwreck. Unfortunately, his premonition came true—both his wife and surviving child drowned in the *City of Columbus* disaster.

Mrs. Caleb Richardson, wife of a prominent Boston businessman, also had a premonition of disaster on the high seas but overcame her fears and sailed aboard the *City of Columbus*. She did not survive.

Then there's the tale of the honeymooners aboard the *City of Columbus*. In the middle of the night of the shipwreck,

> *at the moment, many miles away in New Market, New Hampshire, Nathaniel Bunker woke up screaming from a nightmare. He dreamed he was standing on a high cliff looking down on a large steamship as it hit a reef and began to sink. "I could see men, women and children struggling in the water," he told two of his friends who came to visit him the next morning. "Wreckage was everywhere, and I saw Lou Chase trying to help my daughter into a lifeboat, but a big wave came and swept everything away."*[12]

Just two days earlier, Lou Chase had married Bunker's daughter. The young couple planned their honeymoon aboard the *City of Columbus*. "I know I'll never see my daughter again," cried the old man.

The honeymooners never had a chance.

5
The Crew

The shipwreck of the *City of Columbus* unfolded like a movie in slow motion. While the immediate impact of the ship crunching onto Devil's Bridge awoke most of the passengers, it was nearly a half hour before the ship actually sank. Within that timeframe, almost everyone aboard ship came to anticipate their horrifying fates: most succumbed to drowning or froze to death from hypothermia.

Of the 132 people who sailed into Vineyard Sound on the *City of Columbus* in the fateful early morning hours of January 18, 1884, only 29 made it out alive. It is obviously from the accounts of those 29 that we learn of the confusion aboard ship during its final minutes.

The *City of Columbus* set off from Boston on January 17 with a crew of six officers and thirty-nine able-bodied seamen. Seventeen crew members survived. None of the thirty-five women and children was rescued. Of the dozen passengers who lived, most were young and agile and able to withstand the frigid winds and seemingly endless hours hanging from rigging above the sunken ship.

This was a disaster of classic proportions; everything that could go wrong did. While Captain Wright gratuitously stayed aloft until everyone else had been saved, it was he who not only allowed the ship to founder but also failed to direct his crew to rescue his passengers, which contributed to the catastrophic loss of life.

This scrap of wood, salvaged from the *City of Columbus*, was painted by an unknown artist. Laura Osborn, daughter of an Edgartown whaling captain, had the painting in her possessions. In 1910, Laura married Henry Edson, a dealer in monuments (gravestones); their Edgartown house and furnishings were sold in 1945 to John and Mary Correia, in-laws of Patricia Correia. The Correias brought Edson/Osborn belongings to their camp on the Edgartown–West Tisbury Road, including this piece. It is unknown how the artifact came into the possession of Laura Osborn, who was sixteen when the shipwreck occurred. *Property of Patricia Correia, on loan to the Martha's Vineyard Museum; photograph by Joyce Dresser.*

Captain Wright oversaw the navigational responsibilities on the *City of Columbus* while departing Boston Harbor and heading out into Cape Cod Bay. Navigation of the era was refined, with the steamship route clearly delineated by lighthouses, lightships and buoys, compass and sextant at hand, meticulously measured charts and the experience of a professional pilot like Captain Schulyer Wright. He guided his ship expertly across the expanse of Boston Harbor, out around Provincetown and thence down the eastern shore of Cape Cod.

For fifteen years, Captain Wright had been a licensed pilot. He had held command of the *City of Columbus* with the Boston and Savannah Steamship Company since September 1882. He felt in control of his ship. With West Chop light on the Vineyard off his port bow, he picked up Nobska Light on the starboard, just off Woods Hole, and reset his course in a southwesterly direction, where he could see Tarpaulin Cove light ahead on Naushon Island.

The weather was wintry—cold and windy but no major storm brewing. The moon was in its gibbous phase, six days past full. It rose at 10:30 p.m., and as the night wore on, moonlight illuminated the land and waters, aiding the helmsman as he steered by Monomoy Point, past the Pollock Rip lightship and into Nantucket Sound.

The thermometer had registered just below freezing when the *City of Columbus* left Boston Harbor that afternoon. By the time the *City of Columbus* reached Naushon Island, well after midnight, Captain Wright had been at the helm, on duty, for nearly twelve hours—not necessarily at the wheel but involved in all aspects of navigational activity, noting the ship's location on charts, picking up lighthouse beacons along the way, monitoring tidal flow and observing wind direction and velocity. The ship motored along at ten to twelve knots per hour, riding the ebbing tide. Wright was the pilot, the sole person in charge of the ship; he was the one responsible for anything and everything that happened to the *City of Columbus*.

It was not unusual for the captain to take a break once he had steamed through the challenges of Vineyard Sound, where the tide appears to flood in one direction but ebbs in a slightly different contour. A strong wind will push a ship off course. The longer the stretch for the wind to blow over open water (fetch), the greater the influence of wind on the ship's course. This was often the case in wintry weather, a navigational aspect for which pilots learned to account.

Other ships, many other ships, frequented this waterway, as it was the most efficient route up and then around Cape Cod to Boston prior to the opening of the Cape Cod Canal in 1914. Indeed, that night another ship passed the *City of Columbus* in Vineyard Sound less than an hour before the disaster. A pilot must always be alert and aware of other vessels.

The night was cold. The hour was late. After twelve hours of commanding his ship through the vicissitudes of Cape Cod, Nantucket Sound and Vineyard Sound, Captain Wright felt he needed a break. He described the voyage as one that "continued by East and West Chop with a strong breeze, west southwest. Passed Nobska, and soon after, with course west southwest, I stepped into my room to warm myself. It was very cold. Everything was working well."[13]

Captain Wright felt confident in assigning navigational responsibilities to his second mate, Augustus Harding. The captain assumed Harding would share any instructions with the quartermaster, Roderick McDonald, the man at the wheel. Both men had years of experience at sea, but neither was a

The twenty-foot quarter board from the *City of Columbus* dominates the Martha's Vineyard Museum's shipwreck exhibit. A ship's decorative quarter board named the ship; one sign is placed on each side of the vessel, below the quarterdeck. *Courtesy of Martha's Vineyard Museum; photograph by Paul Cournoyer.*

licensed pilot. They were capable seamen. The ship's lookout, Edward Leary, should have been up to the task of scanning the waters for anything out of the ordinary. The time was appropriate, the captain thought, for him to safely crawl into his pilothouse to rest and warm up for the rest of the voyage.

An editorial noted that "the trouble with old and well seasoned navigating officers is that, as a general rule, they have become so familiar with their routes and courses themselves that they too often take too much knowledge in their inferiors for granted, and place in them altogether too implicitly a confidence."[14] Those comments epitomize the case aboard the *City of Columbus*.

Captain Wright believed he was in his cabin only about twenty minutes; it was at least double that amount of time. Time expands or contracts in the middle of the night, depending on whether one is cold, tired, unsure or insecure in one's surroundings. The captain reported that the night was cold and he needed to warm up. And everything appeared to be "working well."

Before retiring to his room, Captain Wright noted the location of the ship off Nobska Light. He ordered Quartermaster McDonald, the man at the wheel, to "set her course <u>southwest by south</u>."

The conventional route to steer through the channel was west-southwest, which means two points of the compass south of west.

The captain claimed he later directed Second Mate Gus Harding to relay additional instructions to the helmsman to steer "<u>southwest by west</u>." It is quite possible this revised order was not followed and thus led to the disaster.

Southwest by south was the course steered by the *City of Columbus*. Southwest by west was the course change that apparently was not followed.

We have no idea what Second Mate Harding heard or whether he failed to pass on the revised orders. He did not survive to explain whether he even heard the captain. That, in short, may confirm that navigational error led to the shipwreck.

Captain Wright never lay down on his bunk. He stayed fully clothed, seated on the floor, with his head in his hands and his back against the heater in the pilothouse that funneled hot air up from the steam engine below. He was ready to oversee things momentarily, if need be, yet he was out of the wind. It was customary for Captain Wright to duck into his room about this time in the journey. The ship was almost out into open water and would then steam south along the coast. There was nothing to worry about, no reason not to take a break. He was the captain and deserved a little time off. He believed the ship was in good hands.

Captain Wright expressed full confidence in his second mate, Augustus Harding. Wright had promoted Harding from quartermaster to second mate. He felt Harding was seasoned and mature, a man in his late twenties. In reality, Harding was only a few months past twenty-one. Wright had suggested that Harding apply for his pilot's license, but Harding never did. Wright never followed through to see whether Harding had done so or to question why he had not. Captain Wright believed the ship was appropriately supervised, even though Harding was not a licensed pilot.

The day after the disaster, Captain Wright indicated that "it may be possible that the officer in charge did not realize the strong drift that was setting the vessel to leeward."[15] A week after the calamity, it was reported Captain Wright "had twice reprimanded Mr. Harding, the officer in charge of the ship at the time she struck, for altering the course of the vessel without calling his attention to the fact."[16] It was obvious that blame was assigned, though the culprit did not survive the wreck.

Below deck were eight firemen. In shifts, these hardy souls shoveled coal into the furnaces to heat the boilers to maintain steam to power the ship. They were hard at work. With the vessel proceeding at ten knots an hour, there was a lot of coal to shovel to maintain speed. As coal burned, the ship gradually lightened its load, thus traveling slightly higher and faster in the water. That was another variable to be considered in navigation. The firemen, however, were concerned only that they keep the furnaces filled.

The ship *Panther*, of the Philadelphia and Reading line, passed the *City of Columbus* shortly before 3:00 a.m. on Friday morning, headed north through Vineyard Sound en route to Newburyport, on the north shore of Massachusetts. Captain Warrington of the *Panther* reported, "There was a heavy wind blowing and a heavy sea running, both being astern of the *Panther* and ahead of the *City of Columbus*."[17] The captain described what he witnessed:

> The City of Columbus *was about two miles to the starboard, close to the Vineyard shore. The* City of Columbus *should have been in mid channel, as well the* Panther, *as the route eastward and westward is the same, the opening being too narrow to admit of any great leeway with safety.*

It was obvious, a half hour before the disaster, that the *City of Columbus* was off course.

The man at the wheel of the *City of Columbus* lived to recount his activities on that fateful night. Quartermaster Roderick McDonald played a key role as the helmsman, the man who steered the ship into the crisis. He was described by a reporter for the *New Bedford Standard* as "a tall, broad-shouldered Scotchman, with a pleasant, open countenance, and having dark hair and having dark side whiskers, somewhat sprinkled with gray." McDonald came on duty at midnight on January 17, along with Second Mate Gus Harding. Harding relieved First Mate Ed Fuller.

The Sinking of the *City of Columbus*

Among the party who escaped from the wrecked City of Columbus, *to Gay Head, was Roderick A. McDonald, quartermaster, who had charge of the vessel when she struck. He gave the following account of the wreck and the escape of his party: "I went on duty at midnight. During the early part of the night we had heavy winds, but it was clear and we could see the lights plainly, though it was hazy on land. The captain went below about three quarters of an hour before the vessel struck, and gave me the course a quarter or half an hour before he went below. It was southwest by west. The second mate was in the pilot house when the course was given. He told me a short time before she struck not to go to leeward of that course. She might have gone a point or half a point off. She is liable to do so. I steered that course."*[18]

This crucial comment, that the ship may "have gone a point or half a point off," was expanded in his interview with the *New Bedford Standard*: "There was a strong wind blowing nearly ahead and considerable seas; it was quite light on the water, although the land was not clearly visible on account of a sort of fog or haze that hung over it."

So McDonald had trouble making out the land mass on his port bow. The wind had picked up as the ship passed through Vineyard Sound. Considerable seas, or waves, had an impact on the progress and direction of the ship.

McDonald continued, "I thought the light on Gay Head appeared a little closer than usual, but did not attach much importance to the fact, thinking perhaps that the tide rip together with the wind, as we were light, had carried us somewhat to the leeward." In short, McDonald allowed the ship to drift right onto the rocks of the Vineyard because of the wind, the tide and the boat being light in the water. He basically admitted culpability in the disaster. And the acting pilot, Harding, did not pay attention to the deviation in the course.

"The passage in the Vineyard Sound at this point is almost five miles wide, but the tired, over-confident mate did not realize that the combined force of wind and tide near Menemsha Bight was slowly dragging the great steamer to disaster."[19] Edwin Rowe Snow, a twentieth-century historian and expert on shipwrecks, wrote, "It later developed that the man at the wheel, Quartermaster MacDonald, had not heard the low-voiced instruction the captain gave the first mate."[20] (Harding was actually the second mate.)

The *City of Columbus* gently crunched onto the Devil's Bridge and came to a halt a little after 3:30 a.m. on Friday, January 18, 1884. Fireman John Hines was on watch in the fire room, in the middle of his shift, when he felt the ship stop its forward progress. He immediately realized something was amiss.

Purser William Spaulding gave a specific account of what happened:

> *A very few minutes after the vessel struck, she keeled over aft, then shifted her position slightly, as if sliding down off the ledge, and the after part of the ship filled and sank. As the stern went down the vessel righted and the swell carried her head up again on the ledge, when she settled permanently, apparently between boulders or on a bottom.*

The *City of Columbus* literally ran atop a rocky outcropping and became stuck, unable to move ahead. She impaled herself on the Devil's Bridge and became immobile. For several long moments, the sound of the ship grinding against the rock was all anyone could hear.

Captain Wright then gave the fateful order to reverse engines.

The ship's bells rang. Fireman Hines was aware that the captain had switched the ship's direction into reverse, backing up two lengths. Hines did not know whether this meant they had to avoid another vessel or a dangerous reef. Something was wrong, but Fireman Hines continued to shovel coal into the furnaces. No sooner had the ship backed up than the bells rang again, and the ship tried to inch forward. Nothing happened. Hines noted that there was only fifty-seven pounds of pressure in the boiler; the gauge should have registered seventy pounds.

Once the captain reversed direction of the ship, it started to take on water through a hole some three feet in diameter in its bow. (Weeks after the wreck, it was determined that the *City of Columbus* had broken off a large corner of a huge undersea boulder, the Devil's Back; a severed piece of the ledge was discovered on the ocean bottom nearby.)

When he couldn't dislodge the ship with the steam engine, Captain Wright tried a sail. Quartermaster McDonald said:

> *He* [Captain Wright] *gave orders to hoist the jib to cant her head off to westward. There were plenty of men on duty and the sail was set very*

promptly. She swung off a couple of points, and then came back again. She would not back off the reef, and then the captain tried to go over it, ringing ahead full steam. It was no use.[21]

He could not get the ship unstuck from the rocky ledge.

As the ship settled back on the rock, which protruded like the gable of a house, it slowly listed to port, so the left side of the ship's deck heeled over, almost under water.

Second Steward Charles Howes requested his staff to "get the crowd together and if you can't raise them any other way, break in the doors."[22] He added, "I shouted to the passengers to save themselves as well as they could." But when passengers scrambled topside up stairwells or companionways, they were thrown off their feet, bouncing against the walls, losing their balance and sliding down to the deck.

One passenger who had nautical expertise was Captain Hammond of Gouldsboro, Maine. He noted, "[The ship] began to fill forward fast, but as she settled down the stern went under, as the water was deeper aft. At the same time she heeled over, the windward side rising until she was nearly on her beam ends." The 275-foot-long vessel flooded from one end to the other.

This was devastating. The *City of Columbus* righted itself, sitting low in the water, then slowly yawned back and gradually settled into the ocean, sinking stern first. A series of sequential calamities contributed to the disaster, from the gentle crunch on the boulder of Devil's Bridge to the captain's decision to reverse engines to the ship's filling with water, listing to port and then righting itself before sinking backward into the seas with only its two masts above water.

Captain Wright gave his assessment of the crisis: "It was blowing very hard and a heavy sea was running…The sea was breaking over the steamer's deck and the stern being entirely under water, we were forced to go up on top of the houses."[23] He added, "I think the steamer struck a lone rock." It was reported that "the vessel sank in about four fathoms of water and the railing at the bow was the only portion of the hull visible."

Although the *City of Columbus* was fully equipped with six lifeboats and a life raft, as well as sufficient life preservers, more than one hundred people drowned.

Approximately 80 percent of the people aboard ship lost their lives within twenty minutes as the ship foundered on the Devil's Bridge, broadside to the merciless, pounding waves and fierce ocean wind.

Dozens of newspapers editorialized on the disaster. One popular opinion stated:

> *Looking at it in the light of the facts now known we should say that nothing but the grossest carelessness or a criminal recklessness could have put her upon the rocks. The night was clear and the moon was shining—the buoy could be seen at a distance of 300 yards. Gay Head light was in full sight, and although the wind was blowing strongly there seems to have been no excuse whatever for those navigating the ship not to know her exact position every instant of the time she was passing through Vineyard Sound.*[24]

Passenger Hammond was not impressed with the actions of the crew: "I never saw a crew in such utter confusion and disorder." He added, "I do not think there was an order given by the captain after the vessel went on the rocks."

Another experienced voice was that of Captain Frank Howes, of the competing Baltimore line, who told the *Globe* that the night was clear. He spoke to the disaster:

> *Unquestionably, this officer on the deck of the* City of Columbus *did not watch his course, and the wind being a little on his starboard bow and the ship being light, and her propeller racing as was bound to do in the rough sea they must have had, and she not having much speed, it continually kept knocking her about off to the south, or to the left, toward this ledge.*

Another factor was the tide, which pushed the ship farther off course. With the tide ebbing off her starboard bow, the ship tended to drift farther south, farther off course, into and onto the Devil's Bridge. "An eastern tide I saw it was by the almanac," reported Captain Howes. And that tide took the *City of Columbus* aground, and one hundred people lost their lives.

Had Captain Wright been more attentive to the course of his ship, this tragedy could have been averted.

Following is a list of the members of the crew of the *City of Columbus*. Underlined names indicate the seventeen crew members who survived. A few of the crew recalled which lifeboat they were assigned to.

CREW MEMBERS

(underlined names indicate survivors)

Bigney, Daniel: waiter
Boardman, William: waiter
Briggs, Edward: porter
Butler, Thomas: fireman—boat #1
Carney, Thomas: fireman
Clark, Philip: quartermaster
Collins, Henry: second/third engineer
Day, Michael: oiler
Dinn, James: quartermaster
Fitzpatrick, William: pantryman
Fuller, Edwin: first officer
Gallagher, Thomas: second cook
Gallant, Simon: seaman
Hanson, Furber: waiter
Harding, Joseph Augustus: second mate— boat #6 [Gus was born in Chatham on July 7, 1862. His parents were Walden Harding and Julia Ann Cahoon. He was the fourth or middle child, with six siblings. At the time of his death on January 18, 1884, he was twenty-one.]
Hines, John: fireman
Howes, Charles: second steward
Kennedy, Michael: seaman
Leary, Edward: lookout—boat #6
Low, James: oiler
Madden, John: seaman [John was from Charlottetown, Prince Edward Island. He heard the captain or mate say, "We shall lose the poor ship, but don't be alarmed, we will be saved."]
Mahoney, Frank: pantryman
McCarthy, Daniel: baker
McDonald, Daniel: messboy
McDonald, John: messman

McDonald, Roderick: quartermaster—boat #1
McGiggan, Alexander: fireman
McKenna, John: oiler
Morrison, Archibald: chief engineer [Archibald was from Boston, Massachusetts.]
Moore, Harry: waiter
Murray, William: third engineer [William was from Boston, Massachusetts.]
O'Brien, Edward: seaman—boat #3
O'Leary, Cornelius: fireman
O'Leary, Thomas: fireman boat #5
Phillips, HA: first assistant engineer—boat #3
Pitman, Andrew: chief steward—life raft
Roach, John: fireman
Smith, Teresa: stewardess [The only woman on the crew.]
Smith, Michael: fireman
Spaulding, William: purser
Sullivan, Richard: waiter
White, John: seaman—boat #2
Whitehead, John: cook/chief cook [John's body was identified by his wife and brother, who came up from New York.]
Wright, Schuyler: captain

44 total (one name missing)

It was noted that a George Carr, age nineteen, told friends he planned to work his passage aboard a vessel headed south. It was "feared he may be the unnamed member of the crew already mentioned as lost."[25] Carr would bring the crew total to forty-five.

6

The Passengers

The passenger list of the *City of Columbus* was a representative sample of people who dwelt in the northeastern United States in the late 1800s. A few small children were aboard, as well as two sets of teenage brothers and several young adults traveling with their parents. Numerous passengers fell into the category of senior citizens or people traveling south for the winter for their health. And there were a few businessmen on board. This varied collection of people meant that the crew had to meet the needs of several age groups.

The *City of Columbus* was long but narrow, with a beam of just under forty feet, so the decks served more as corridors than as quadrants. Staterooms were centered midship, so passengers became acquainted as roommates or neighbors and congregated in the Social Hall, dining saloons or various other meeting places aboard ship.

When the *City of Columbus* departed from Boston's Nickerson Wharf in midafternoon on Thursday, January 17, 1884, it was ushered out to sea with good wishes from relatives and friends of the eighty-seven passengers. The fortnightly steamship sailings out of Boston were routine, so it was not unusual for well-wishers to attend the departure.

It was mid-January, with freezing temperatures and only an hour or so left of daylight as the vessel steamed out of the harbor. Excitement at exchanging the blustery chill of Boston for the warmth of Savannah brought exuberance to the ship's passengers. And the luxurious appointments of the vessel, from elegant inlaid rosewood panels to rich embroidered cushions, impressed the voyagers with a sense of security and empowerment on their journey.

The *City of Columbus* steamed along at ten to twelve miles per hour, according to a *Scientific American* report, when it was launched in 1878. *Courtesy of the Mariner's Museum, Newport News, Virginia.*

"Dining accommodations aboard the *Columbus* filled the breadth of the cabin at the foot of the broad stairway which led down from the Social Hall to the Grand Saloon."[26] Long dining tables were set off by couches with soft, plush cushions. Revolving chairs were opposite. It was an impressive display for elegant dining.

According to John Cook, fellow passengers quickly befriended one another before dinner and anticipated a relaxing three-day journey. "Strangers unbent to each other in their first hours aboard ship."[27] Friendliness and cheerfulness among the passengers was evident. The description continued: "No lighthearted, happier crowd ever sailed from port." Another passenger, Fred Tibbetts, noted, "In the middle of the northern winter they were bound for summer land." Tibbetts appreciated the "spacious public rooms" and "his commodious stateroom."

"It was a jolly evening aboard ship," Mr. Tibbetts recalled. "The saloons and smoking rooms were filled 'til quite a late hour."[28]

The evening meal, the sole meal served, was a sumptuous repast. A menu from the previous year survives to suggest an array of delicate delicious delights served aboard ship.[29] It was a feast of elegance, at least for first-class passengers.

Mock turtle soup or mutton broth opened the meal. This was followed by baked white anchovies with sauce, a choice of rib beef with gravy or turkey with cranberry sauce, corned beef mutton with caper sauce and an entree

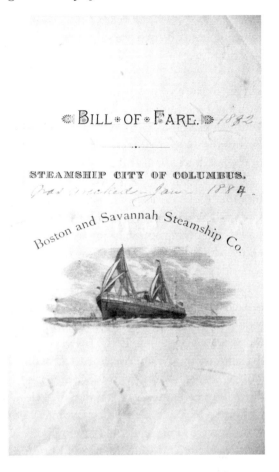

The bill of fare from the *City of Columbus* offered a sumptuous repast of dietary delights. The dining experience aboard this elegant vessel was integral to its appeal. *Courtesy of Richard Boonisar; photograph by Thomas Dresser.*

of thin-cut calf's head on toast. To accompany this delight, the chef offered mashed or baked potatoes and spinach or green peas with relishes of celery, jellied beets and pickles. Squash or blueberry pie, with apples, oranges and grapes, was available for dessert. It was noted that the waiter kept his pencil handy to add special requests. The passengers aboard the *City of Columbus* ate well. For many, this was their last supper.

With anticipation of two more full days at sea, most passengers retired to bed by 10:00 p.m. Dinner had been enjoyable, but the excitement of boarding the boat in Boston, appreciating the steamship's progress through the waning hour of daylight and becoming acclimated to the unique surroundings, not to mention fellow passengers, used up a good deal of energy.

Virtually all passengers, and most of the forty-five-member crew, were asleep when the *City of Columbus* steamed into Vineyard Sound in the early morning hours. When the ship struck, most of the crew and passengers were in a deep sleep.

Shortly after 3:30 a.m., in the deepest hour of night, John Cook, a screen maker from Portland, Maine, awoke in his stateroom berth. He realized something was wrong and tried to wake his roommate, a man from Brunswick, Maine, perhaps a Mr. N.D. Eaton. The roommate was stunned by the crash, "seemed crazed" by the incident, as Cook recalled, and perished in the harsh waters.

John Weidmann, of Lawrence, was in his stateroom. He aroused his roommate, Frederick Sargent of Merrimac, Massachusetts. Weidmann survived; Sargent did not. Weidmann shared the recollection of leaving his stateroom, noting a man trying to calm a woman and two young boys, intent on reducing the element of panic that surrounded them. None of that party was seen again.

Another passenger, G.I. Whitcomb of Hudson, Massachusetts, was in steerage. He was one of the few steerage passengers to survive. His roommate, George Goddard of Stowe, did not. Mr. Whitcomb recounted that as the tragedy unfolded, "I saw a man and a woman come out of one of the staterooms and after talking to each other in loud tones at the same time looking at each other with long, lingering looks of love and endearment, they embraced and kissed tenderly."[30] Whitcomb continued, "I went out on the upper deck and heard the captain cry down the stairs, 'Don't be afraid,' at the same instant he turned to somebody and said, 'We shall have to leave the poor thing,' meaning the vessel I presumed."

Captain Wright and his crew had little or no time to alert passengers or prepare them for the unfolding catastrophe. Andrew F. Pitman, chief steward, said, "As the women and children came on deck they were swept overboard by the scores and the scene was terrible."[31] Another account, given by Second Assistant Engineer Henry Collins, stated that "passengers from the main saloon were crowding on deck and were being washed overboard as fast as they came up the companionway."

Purser William Spaulding offered his observations:

Men and women, some with children in their arms, clambered up to the deck, clinging frantically to every available projection that offered resistance. They crowded upon each other so fast that they could not be counted as they rushed upon the deck, only to be met by some monstrous wave and swept off into the sea. Groans, yells and curses contended with the fury of the gale. Women shrieked and men shouted themselves hoarse. Men and women clutched each other regardlessly, shouting all the while, and struggling with each other in frenzied attempts to secure every edge of vantage.

The purser realized this was a most traumatic moment: "But this soul-rending sight could not last long. Sea after sea swept over the ship carrying off everything that was not made of iron."[32] He added, "Many of the passengers were swept overboard as soon as they came on deck."

A widely circulated tabloid account of the disaster included this traumatic description: "Waves were dashing over the decks, and within twenty minutes every woman and child had been swept away. No human power could save them."[33] The story went on: "Wives threw their arms around their husbands' necks, bade them good-by for ever, and a few moments afterwards both were carried away. One mother, with her child clasped tightly in her arm, was borne off almost before reaching the top of the stairs."

This graphic illustration on the cover of the *National Police Gazette* epitomized how tabloid newspapers seized on the tragedy. The *Police Gazette* was founded in 1845 and featured illustrations that challenged the propriety of the Victorian age. *Photo courtesy of Eric Takakjian/Quest Marine Services.*

Captain Hammond, the passenger with nautical expertise, reported that "many had been drowned in the cabin, and as water poured into the windows and openings on the side and rushed aft in a great wave, furniture, baggage, freight, and an occasional body would float out. It was a terrible sight, and was particularly sickening as we felt that our turn might come at any minute."

Of the eighty-seven passengers, eleven were children. There were twenty-four women and fifty-two men aboard the ship. Nine married couples were part of this contingent.

Of the eighty-seven passengers, ten came from Canada, and five were heading home to the South. The majority of passengers, fifty-one, were from Massachusetts, with twenty-six from the immediate environs of Boston. Nine passengers hailed from Maine and ten from other New England states. Two passengers had no listed address.

Of the eighty-seven passengers, 80 percent were from New England, 11 percent from Canada, 6 percent from the South and 3 percent unknown. Fully 40 percent were women and children.

Of the eighty-seven passengers, at least five were African American. In the passenger roster, the following were listed as "colored": Jonas Cooper, Theodore Hagan and William Lapham and his two children, for whom both the names and gender are lost.

Sixteen passengers were in steerage; seven were known to survive: Brown, Fairbanks, the Farnsworth brothers, McGarry, Waterhouse and Whitcomb.

The following list of passengers is arranged with survivors' names underlined. Brief details offer background data. If known, the stateroom or steerage category is listed.

PASSENGERS

ATKINSON, ALICE MAUDE MRS. JOHN, thirty, was from Woodstock, New Brunswick. She was recently widowed and was traveling with her son, Wilmot, and nephew, Richard. They were in stateroom fifteen.

ATKINSON, WILMOT L., eight, was from Woodstock, New Brunswick.

BARTLETT, DR. AND MRS. HORCE, were from Lyndon, Vermont. The Bartletts were traveling to Florida for the wife's health. Property of the Bartletts— three nice dresses, two pairs of pantaloons, a vest and Horce's medicine case—was found on the shore by Moses West of Chilmark. They were in stateroom seven.

BATCHELDER, MR. AND MRS. HENRY, forty-five, lived at 16 Everett Avenue in Dorchester. Henry was a retired coal merchant. They were traveling south to care for his invalid wife, Sarah Brown, a New England heiress. His body was found with a gold watch and chain, a shirt stud and fifty-one dollars in cash. The couple is buried at Forest Hills Cemetery in Boston, Massachusetts. They were in stateroom twenty-one.

BEACH, MISS ELIZABETH, was a minister's daughter, from Mansfield, Connecticut. She was headed to St. Augustine, Florida, as she was in poor health from work at the McAll Mission in Paris. Her estate filed a suit with the owners of the ship. She was in room number ten.

BEAL, MISS INEZ, eighteen, was from Mattapan and shared room twenty-six with her mother.

BEAL, MRS. JAMES, was from Mattapan. She was to join her husband, James Beal, who had journeyed south three months earlier. The Beals had recently lost three of their four children. He had a premonition of this disaster. Mr. Beal had to travel up from Florida to identify the bodies of his wife and daughter. Letters from Mr. Beal were found. She was in stateroom twenty-six.

BELL, MR. CHARLES, was from Hollis, New Hampshire, and was in stateroom I.

BELYEA, MR. AND MRS. ROBERT BAYARD, were from Woodstock, New Brunswick. His brother, A.S. Belyea (whose wife had died earlier that week), was a steward on another steamer. He had to identify the couple, niece Alice Atkinson, Wilmot (known as Mertie), eight, and Coburn, five. They were in stateroom fifteen.

BROOKS, HELON, was a Unitarian from Northborough. Brooks retired from a large manufacturer of piano and organ stops; his health necessitated his withdrawal from the business. "The church was well filled" at his funeral. He was in room number twelve.

BROWN, JAMES, was from Lawrence, Massachusetts. Brown was a former saloonkeeper headed south to work as a carpenter. He was one of the last passengers to register for the trip; he brought a lawsuit for suffering endured during the shipwreck. He was in steerage.

CHASE, MRS. AND MRS. A, were from South Newmarket, New Hampshire. This recently married couple had planned a honeymoon aboard the ship. They were in stateroom A.

COOK, JOHN, was a screen maker from Portland, Maine. He was in stateroom thirty. His roommate, from Brunswick, Maine, was stunned by the crash, "crazed" and perished.

COOPER, JONAS, was listed as a colored boy of Windsor, Vermont. He planned to join his mother in Tallahassee, Florida. He was in stateroom H.

CUMMINGS, ANDREW, seventy, was from Watertown, Massachusetts. He was a widow with three children. He was traveling south to visit his son. He was in stateroom thirty-two.

DANIELS, MRS. C.E., from Lawrence, Massachusetts, was traveling with her son, Henry, on a pleasure trip to Jacksonville, Florida. Her husband was a supervisor at the Pemberton Mills in Lawrence. They were in stateroom twenty-three.

DANIELS, HENRY, eighteen, was from Lawrence, Massachusetts.

DAVIS, MISS ELIZABETH, from Lynn, was an unmarried housekeeper who was planning to find work in Crescent City, Florida. She was in room six.

DURLAND, HOWARD, was from Yarmouth, Nova Scotia. He was in stateroom B.

EATON, N.D., was from Hermon, Maine. Four trunks belonging to N.D. Eaton of Appalachiacola and E.F.H. of Pomona, Florida, were found. He was in stateroom thirty-two.

FAIRBANKS, F.W., was from Gorham, Maine. Fairbanks survived in the rigging with Captain Wright. He was in steerage.

FARNSWORTH, GEORGE, fourteen, was from Townsend, Massachusetts. He was in steerage.

FARNSWORTH, HUBBARD, seventeen, was from Townsend, Massachusetts. He was in steerage.

FAWCETT, SAMPSON, was from Lawrence, Massachusetts. Fawcett's father, Samuel, brought a lawsuit against the Boston and Savannah Steamship Company. He was in steerage.

FROST, CHARLES, was from Natick, Massachusetts. He was in room I.

GIDDINGS, FRANK, was from Nashua, New Hampshire. He was in steerage.

GIVEN, MRS. JAMES, was from Billtown, Nova Scotia. Hallie Given was a nurse traveling with Elizabeth Beach to Florida. She was in stateroom ten.

Two embroidered chairs were salvaged from the shipwreck. The chairs were elegantly covered and still serviceable after all these years. *Property of John and Katie Hough; used with permission of Madeline and Jake Scott. Photograph by Joyce Dresser.*

GODDARD, GEORGE, was from Stowe, Massachusetts. He was in steerage.

GRIFFIN, CLARENCE OR CHARLES, was from Cornwallis/Millbury, Nova Scotia. Griffin was headed south, looking for work. He was in steerage.

HAGAN, THEODORE, was from Boston. He was in stateroom D.

HALE, FREDERICK L., was from Somerville, Massachusetts. Hale was a produce dealer. The Boston Produce Exchange eulogized him at his service. He was thirty-seven years old and left a wife and three children behind. He was on a business trip. He was in room five.

HAMMOND, G. FRED, was from Hyde Park, Massachusetts. He worked as a salesman for Chandler & Company and was rescued by Rhodes but died. He was en route to visit his sister.[34] He was called a "young man of marked ability." He was in room G.

HAMMOND, CAPTAIN THOMAS, was from Gouldsboro, Maine. The week following the wreck, he took the *Gate City* to Savannah. He was in room nineteen.

HEAVER, JOHN, was from Taunton, Massachusetts. He was in steerage.

HINDS, G., was from Lawrence, Massachusetts. He was in steerage.

HUTCHINSON, ALICE, was from Cape Elizabeth, Maine. She was under two years old.

HUTCHINSON, MR. AND MRS. EDWIN, were from Cape Elizabeth, Maine. At age thirty-five, Edwin was unidentified person number eighteen. His body was found with $1.51 and three baggage checks. His wife Alice was twenty-five. The couple and their infant daughter, Alice, planned to relocate to Florida and farm the land. They were in room eighteen.

IASIGI, OSCAR, thirty-seven, lived at 129 Marlboro Street in Boston. He was the son of an Armenian merchant ship owner and had served as Turkish consul general for seven years. He was treasurer of Vassalborough Woolen Mills and was well known in the mercantile community. Iasigi planned to fish for tarpon in Florida. He left behind a wife and two children. His brother, A.D. Iasigi, hired a tug to search for Oscar. Iasigi booked stateroom eleven.

JAMES, CHARLES, was from Natick or Everett, Massachusetts. He was a housepainter. A purse with fifteen dollars and a gold ring, belonging to James, was found at the home of Charles Mingo. James died on the shore of Menemsha; four others in the lifeboat survived. He was in room twenty-two.

KELLOGG, GEORGE, was from Fitchburg, Massachusetts. Kellogg was a job printer and former chairman of the Democratic Senatorial Committee. His body was found at Gay Head with $18.26 and a gold watch, which had stopped at 7:23 a.m. He was in room six.

KELLOGG, MRS. H.B., fifty-eight, lived at 9 Park Square in Boston. She left the Women's Education and Industrial Union to keep house for or be the guest of the U.S. district attorney E.M. Cheney in Florida. She was in stateroom sixteen.

KELLY, BRIDGET ELLEN, was from Atlanta, Georgia. She was the young daughter of Anne Kelly.

KELLY, MRS. JAMES, was from Atlanta, Georgia. Anne Kelly booked passage in steerage with her daughter, Bridget Ellen. They were headed south to meet her policeman husband. The *Morning Mercury* reported that Policeman Kelly, in Florida, was "bitten by rapid [*sic*] dog and died from hydrophobia."

LAPHAM, WILLIAM, was from Boston. An affidavit was found following the 1953 tornado regarding him and his two children. They were in stateroom D.

LAWRENCE, CAPTAIN LEVI, was from Fitchburg or Ashby, Massachusetts. Captain Lawrence served in the Fifty-seventh Regiment, during the Civil War, and was honorably discharged in 1864. He was in stateroom six.

MAY, FRANK, was from Boston Highlands, Massachusetts. May graduated from the Massachusetts Institute of Technology and was a government employee. As a civil engineer, he had worked on the Boston sewer system; now he was en route to survey the Savannah River. He was in room twenty-eight.

McGARRY, EUGENE, was from Somerville, Massachusetts. He jumped from the rigging and was saved by Lieutenant Rhodes. He was in steerage.

McGARRY, HENRY, was from Somerville, Massachusetts. Both McGarrys were bricklayers by trade. He was in steerage.

MERRILL, JAMES, forty-eight, lived at 225 Washington Street in Roxbury/ Boston. Merrill was a merchant tailor. He was in room twenty-two.

MERRILL, RICHARD COBURN, five, was from Skowhegan, Maine. As in the case of the Rands, five members of his family died in the shipwreck. Besides Coburn, his aunt Alice Maude Atkinson; her son, Wilmot; and Coburn's grandparents, Mr. and Mrs. Robert Belyea, all perished. They were booked in room fifteen.

MITCHELL, D.W., was in room twenty-seven.

MORTON, NATHANIEL, was from Boston. Morton was a *Boston Globe* reporter, formerly with the *Morning Mercury*. He was supposed to sail on the *Gate City*

This sugar bowl was in the original silver service aboard the *City of Columbus*. It washed ashore, was reengraved with details of the wreck and was presented to a Mrs. C.F. Crocker five months after the tragedy. *Courtesy of Martha's Vineyard Museum; photograph by Joyce Dresser.*

but, when assigned a stateroom with a stranger, decided to go with the *City of Columbus*. The *Globe* sent a globe of white carnations to his funeral, inscribed: "We all miss thee." He was in room twelve.

NOURSE, JOEL, eighty-one, was from Boston, Massachusetts. He was an original proprietor of the New England Farmer. According to *Frank Leslie's Illustrated News*, he was a "famous maker of agriculture implements," and he "manufactured almost the first cast-iron plough." A satchel belonging to Joel Nourse was found with family records and diaries. He was in room K.

PEARSON/PIERSON, AUGUST, was from Taunton. Pierson was unidentified person number twenty. He traveled in steerage. Augustus Pierson was a native of England; he had spent five years in the States.

PINKHAM, MRS. SARAH, forty-eight, was from Dover, New Hampshire. She was a widow with a son and a daughter. She was moving to Sanford, Florida, to live with her son. She was in room C.

RAND, REVEREND AND MRS. CHARLES, were from Haverhill, Massachusetts. Reverend Rand was the elected dean of Episcopal clergy and rector of the Trinity Episcopal Church in Haverhill. He and his wife were traveling with their daughter and his parents. "The sweeping away of five from one family is one of the saddest features of the wreck."[35] The five Rands were headed to Florida to visit Charles's brother, who ran an orange grove. They were in room thirteen.

RAND, MR. AND MRS. EDWARD, were from Boston, Massachusetts. Again, according to *Frank Leslie's Illustrated News*, Edward was "one of the older members of the Suffolk bar." He was in the Harvard class of 1828. The *Mercury* noted that a trunk was found belonging to Mr. Rand. Rand, seventy-five, was in poor health, and "a southern trip was deemed advisable." They were in room two.

RAND, MISS FRANCES, was from Haverhill, Massachusetts. Frances was either eight or twelve years old.

RICH, MRS. DWIGHT, fifty-nine, was from Hyde Park, Massachusetts. Mrs. Dwight Rich was headed to Florida "to obtain particulars on her husband's death in 1882," perhaps to visit his grave. She was said to be a guest of Captain Wright. She left behind five children.

RICHARDSON, MR. AND MRS. CALEB, were from Everett, Massachusetts. Caleb Richardson was one of the more prominent taxpayers in Everett. He was a well-known Mason and a successful Boston beef merchant. Mrs. Richardson had a premonition of disaster. They were in room seventeen.

SARGENT, FREDERICK, was from Merrimac, Massachusetts. He was in room thirty-one.

SKENE, MISS ELIZA, was from Tewksbury, Massachusetts. She was in room nine.

SLADE, MRS. HENRY, was from Chelsea, Massachusetts. She was in room fourteen.

SMALL, DARIUS K., was from Beaufort, South Carolina. He was a two-and-a-half-year-old child.

SMALL, MRS. DARIUS K., twenty-three, was from Beaufort, South Carolina. Lillie Small had been visiting her in-laws in Chatham on Cape Cod for several months with her young son. She was in room nine.

SMITH, SUSAN, was from Atlanta, Georgia. She was in steerage.

TIBBETTS, FRED, forty-three, was from Somerville, Massachusetts. Tibbetts ran an express service and was headed south to check on property in Silver Springs, Florida. He and Frank May shared stateroom twenty-eight.

VANCE, CAPTAIN SHERRINGTON, twenty-five, was from North Truro, Nova Scotia. Vance was headed to South America to captain a sailing ship. He filed a lawsuit to recover damages from the wreck. His suit was in conjunction with that of James Brown. He was in stateroom nineteen.

WALKER, JAMES, was from Lawrence, Massachusetts. He was in steerage.

WATERHOUSE, HORACE, was from Bath, Maine. He was in steerage.

WEIDMAN, JOHN, was from Lawrence, Massachusetts. He was in stateroom thirty-one.

WHITCOMB, G.I., was from Hudson, Massachusetts. He was in steerage. His roommate was Goddard, who did not survive.

WHITCOMB, MRS. PERRINTHY A., was from Boston Highlands, Massachusetts. She was in room twenty-six.

WILLET, C.G., was from Canning, Nova Scotia. Willett, a steerage passenger, was said to be a fugitive murderer from Kelland, Nova Scotia. He left behind a widow and children. He was listed as currently a resident of Kingston, New York.

WRIGHT, MR. AND MRS. LYNN. He was a teller at the Lynn Institution of Savings. His wife, also lost, was a native of the Cape. Services were delayed in the hopes of finding Mrs. Wright's body.

WRIGHT, MR. AND MRS. WALLACE, were from Lynn, Massachusetts. Mrs. Wallace's first name was Kate. They were in steerage.

WRIGHT, WILLIAM, forty, was from Nashua, New Hampshire. He was a banker and a Sunday school supervisor. He had bought land in Florida. He was in room one.

7
The Shrouds

The word "shroud" has two meanings. Aboard ship, shrouds are lines to secure a mast to the sides of the ship in a stable, balanced manner. In another context, shrouds refer to the cloth used to bury the dead.

Captain Wright reversed engines in an attempt to back his ship off the rocky ledge. Unable to move forward again, he realized his ship was wedged on the rocks and would founder. He had no choice but to abandon ship.

Instead of directing his crew to lower lifeboats and provide a means to rescue his frightened passengers, Captain Wright stepped below and individually assisted passengers with their life preservers. Calmly, he informed people that the ship had run aground and would have to be abandoned.

Meanwhile, the *City of Columbus* sat broadside to the seas, acting as a great sail facing an intense northwest wind. It was out of the protection, or the lee, of the Elizabeth Islands of Vineyard Sound. Over the long fetch of open water, the gale stirred up massive combers, waves that lashed the ship mercilessly.

Able-bodied seamen struggled valiantly to release lifeboats, load them with passengers and launch them into the forbidding seas. Either the crew could not loosen the lines from the davits, which secured the boats, or worried that missing plugs (used to allow rainwater to drain from the lifeboats) would cause the boats to sink. The crew could not get the boats freed. When the *City of Columbus* heeled to port, those lifeboats became useless, as they were either submerged or smashed against the hull of the ship. Crew members then sought to launch lifeboats from the starboard side but met with little luck.

The *City of Columbus* heeled over, temporarily righted itself and then sank, stern first, into the frigid waters. It took less than half an hour. And it was four o'clock in the morning.

The disaster assumed horrendous proportions as frightened passengers, stampeding up the companionways, were quickly washed off the ship's deck into the frigid waters and to their deaths.

"The scenes on the wreck, as she lay beaten by the waves in the darkness of the bitterly cold Winter's morning, were pathetic and terrible beyond description."[36] There was no time to prepare passengers for the unfolding catastrophe. Captain Wright did not respond as if it were an emergency but urged calm preparation for departing the ship. One stark statement reported that "the majority of the passengers were at once swept into the sea and perished."[37]

The following week, *Frank Leslie's Illustrated News*[38] revisited the fear and horror of the disaster, describing a crisis where passengers began to buckle their life preservers even as powerful waves broke over the deck: "The water filled the state rooms and cabin slowly, and there was the continual pounding of the vessel on the ledge, but the full extent of the danger was not realized. Within twenty minutes, however, all below decks became untenable, and then the real horrors began." One wave was said to pull sixty people off the deck at once.

The victims washed into the seas succumbed to hypothermia, which occurs when body temperature falls below ninety-five degrees. In the water, heat is lost from the body more rapidly than in air. The natural reaction is to try to swim, to thrash about seeking help, but that induces the loss of more body heat.

Initially, hypothermia causes shivering, lethargy and loss of muscle control. The person may appear incoherent or combative. Imagine a woman, in her nightclothes, washed into the ocean, where rescue was virtually impossible.

Moderate hypothermia occurs within a few minutes of immersion in cold water. It would induce delirium, in which the brain cannot comprehend the need to survive. A person would make an inappropriate response to the conditions—for example, jumping out of a lifeboat, fearing the boat would sink. In the ocean, the person drowns.

This rendering of the wreck (based on the photograph in chapter one) was painted by Edmund Russell (1851–1927). It is the property of Peter McGhee. The painting hung at the farmhouse at Quansoo for many years; Mr. McGhee had it cleaned and reframed. Of the artist, Mr. McGhee writes, "Russell was from West Tisbury. He went whaling out of Edgartown as a young man, making three arctic voyages, then studied art in New York and eventually worked as a sign painter in New Bedford and then South Dartmouth, where he set up his own business in 1893 and lived for the rest of his life." *On loan to the shipwreck exhibit at the Martha's Vineyard Museum; photograph by Joyce Dresser.*

Severe hypothermia causes respiratory distress, cardiac arrest and unconsciousness or coma. With ocean water pouring into the submerged staterooms, passengers who could not escape may have become comatose and appeared dead; their bodies floated away. Descriptions of such scenes were part of the trauma. Anyone washed into the ocean would suffer from hypothermia if not pulled out quickly and warmed.

In January, when the water temperature was probably forty degrees, passengers from the *City of Columbus* had little chance of survival.

In extremely cold ocean water, the very young and very old are more susceptible to hypothermia because they are less equipped to generate body heat. Only a few minutes in the water can be fatal. Women and children of the late nineteenth century were not particularly agile or nimble; exercise was not part of their regime. Hence, they were less capable of saving themselves. This immediate, unanticipated exposure to very cold water and freezing air temperatures induced hypothermia in many of the 103 people who died in the shipwreck.

The crew managed to launch two lifeboats.

Several passengers clambered aboard the first lifeboat to hit the water, only to have it capsize, drowning them in the frigid seas. One passenger, Captain Sherrington Vance, found himself beneath the capsized lifeboat, managed to right it, climbed in, capsized again and was found unconscious later that day by the tug *Speedwell*. When the tug returned to Vineyard Haven Harbor that evening, Captain Vance managed to walk ashore with minimal assistance, although he had spent over nine hours in the open seas, semiconscious in a swamped lifeboat.

Three people were in another lifeboat when Quartermaster Roderick McDonald joined them. Those three, who included stewardess Theresa Smith, jumped out, fearing the lifeboat would sink. They drowned.

McDonald assumed control of the lifeboat as four others—Edmund Leary (lookout), James Brown (passenger), Charles F. James (passenger) and Simon Gallant (seaman)—clambered over the gunnels. The five men rowed and drifted toward shore. McDonald urged them to head farther north, beyond the rocky coast by the Gay Head cliffs, where breakers were smashing against the shore. They made landfall after three hours, reaching shore near Menemsha. The men crawled out of the boat and struggled up a pathway to the house of a Native American woman named Ryan.

An account of this struggle reads, [39] "A battered lifeboat had drifted ashore about a mile down the beach toward Lobsterville. Four half-dead men stumbled onto the sand and collapsed there. One of them saw a well worn wagon road and staggered up it until he reached a small house."

McDonald explained, "Afterwards, I got up to a house with Ned Leary and Giand [Gallant] and the occupants who were named Ryan." Passenger James Brown had frostbitten feet.

The tale continued:

> *Mrs. Rachel Diamond Ryan was in her kitchen, baking some biscuits, when she heard a faint shout. She ran to the door and found a man lying unconscious on the doorstep. With the help of her husband Charles, they dragged him inside. Revived, he told his story and help was sent to the others on the shore. One of the men had died and his body was carried into Conant Jeffers' fish shack, where it was laid gently on a pile of fish net.*

Charles James was the victim who expired on the beach of Menemsha. Besides Captain Vance, McDonald, Leary, Brown and Gallant were the only people to survive the wreck on their own.

More crew members, some with rank, climbed onto the life raft and drifted away from the sinking steamer. Although the raft was supposed to accommodate as many as forty people, only a half dozen men were aboard: Archibald Morrison, chief engineer; Edwin Fuller, first mate; Augustus Harding, second mate; William Murray, assistant engineer; William Fitzpatrick, pantryman; and Richard Sullivan, waiter. They believed they could make it to shore on the raft.

Those passengers and crew who were not washed off the decks, yet were unable or unwilling to board lifeboats, hoisted themselves up into the rigging of the masts, the only points of the ship still above water. As the disaster unfolded, as many as forty men managed to pull themselves aloft into the shrouds or rigging in the two masts above the sinking ship.

Over the course of several hours, many men hung on to the shrouds. The onset of civil twilight on January 18, 1884, was 6:36 a.m., with sunrise at 7:06 a.m. That meant that after more than two hours aloft, the men in the rigging could make out images on the shore or in the water, which indicated daylight was not far off.

Descriptions of their ordeal were captured in weekly tabloids. "Soon after daybreak the smokestack was carried away."[40] Of the men clinging to the rigging in the masts, a reporter wrote, "The gale swung them back and forth like clothes upon a clothesline, while the spray of every wave breaking over the ship drenched them."

The harrowing experience of the men in the masts cannot be overplayed. One shipwreck authority shared the drama of the disaster. His poignant phrase captures the crisis of the men hanging on for their lives: "Frozen onto the shrouds because of the surf which lashed around them, and numbed by the zero wind which swept through their thin garments."[41] At least a dozen men either froze to death in the rigging or dropped to the sea from weariness. Many who had managed to hoist themselves into the rigging plunged to their deaths from exhaustion, hypothermia or fright before rescue arrived.

One sign of hope for the men in the rigging was that the light from the Gay Head lighthouse was briefly obscured, as if the keeper were sending a signal—which indeed Horatio Pease was. When lighthouse keeper Pease caught sight of the men in the ship's shrouds in the early morning light, he threw a blanket over the light to send a signal that they were seen and help was on the way.

Another hopeful sign appeared on the horizon about 8:00 a.m., four hours after the wreck. Some twenty-eight men were still aloft in the main rigging at that time, and another five clung to the forward mast. Shortly after daybreak, the steamer *Glaucus* entered Vineyard Sound from the south. Captain Maynard Bearse of the *Glaucus* focused his telescope on the wreck. He confirmed that it was the *City of Columbus*, as he noted in the subsequent inquiry, "No ships leaving Boston carry their smoke stack so far forward as the Savannah boats."

However, neither he nor his crew claimed to have seen anyone waving or hanging from the rigging.

Author Edwin Rowe Snow, an expert on historical shipwrecks along the New England coast, considered Bearse's dismissive comments to be "lame and impotent." He said that "it was because of a deplorable dullness of mind and vision" that the *Glaucus* failed to at least steam a little closer to the wreck to verify there were no survivors.

Aloft in the rigging of the *City of Columbus*, Purser William Spaulding averred that the crew "could not help seeing us, but which passed without any notice being taken of us."

Later, it was reported that "the *Glaucus* passed in such plain sight that the form of her flag could be seen, and a feeling of discouragement replaced the first one of hope when the steamer continued on her course."[42]

Rescue was still hours off. The gale continued its intensity. The masts of the wreck rocked in the wind. Cold air chilled the men through and through. The waters below were forbidding. The disaster extended well into the morning hours.

8
The Rescue

Native Americans of Martha's Vineyard, the Wampanoags, have many legends of their land. The great ledge off Gay Head has always been of interest. Legend tells of a Wampanoag ancestor, Moshup, who wanted to build a bridge to Cuttyhunk, an island across Vineyard Sound. Moshup lugged big boulders to the shore, waded out into the ocean and began to build his bridge. Along came a crab and bit Moshup's toe. Startled and angry, Moshup dropped his rocks into the sea, and there they lay. That became known as Moshup's Bridge.

Years later, white men came to the Vineyard as missionaries, intent on converting the Wampanoags to Christianity. They introduced the concept of the devil, unknown in Wampanoag lore. Over the years, the legend of Moshup's Bridge was Anglicized. The story evolved that the devil challenged Moshup, saying he, the devil, could build a bridge across the sound to Cuttyhunk overnight, before the cock crowed. Moshup feared the devil would win. In the middle of the night, Moshup went out and found a cock, and then he lit a candle. When the cock saw the candle, he crowed. The devil lost his bet and tossed the rocks into the waters—thus the origin of the Devil's Bridge.

Once the *City of Columbus* foundered on this rocky ledge, Devil's Bridge assumed a more fatal meaning.

At daybreak on the morning of Friday, January 18, assistant light keeper Fred Poole noticed the masts of the *City of Columbus* poking up from the sea a half mile offshore. Recognizing a wreck, he immediately roused his supervisor, Horatio Pease. Pease responded promptly. "The neighborhood was aroused. At daybreak I put a sheet over the light as a signal."[43]

By alerting the community, he summoned help to rescue the stranded crew and passengers of the ship. Putting a sheet over the light indicated that help was on the way. Captain Wright later noted that the signal brought hope to the men clinging to the rigging of the masts.

The *Vineyard Gazette* commended the efforts of lighthouse keeper Pease.[44] Besides alerting the Humane Society volunteers of the wreck and signaling with his light, Horatio Pease also directed the launch of the rescue boats while "attending to a thousand and one other details which there is not space to mention."

Over the course of the morning hours, four lifeboats (one boat going out twice) were launched from Gay Head in an effort to rescue survivors from the sunken steamer.

When the first volunteers arrived, a lifeboat was launched at 7:30 a.m. The Humane Society boat was twenty-seven feet long and six feet wide. Joseph Peters, a whaleboat steerer, was in charge. The crew consisted of Samuel Haskins, Samuel Anthony, John P. Vanderhoop and brothers James and Moses Cooper. All were Wampanoags and members of the Massachusetts Humane Society.

According to the *Vineyard Gazette*, "The wind was blowing fresh from the southwest, and there was a heavy swell." The men were in such a hurry to get underway that they neglected to bring life jackets. James Cooper removed his new leather boots, fearful of damage from the salt spray; he thought his woolen socks would be sufficient. The boat returned at 10:00 a.m. with seven survivors from the wreck.

An attempt was made to launch a whale (seine) boat. Unfortunately, the rugged surf overturned that boat, and it was smashed on the rocky shore; it never made it out to sea. The crew of that whaleboat included Thomas and Henry Jeffers, John Lula, Charles Stevens and Simeon Devine.

When the first boat returned, it was emptied of survivors and replaced by a second crew of volunteers. James Mosher was in charge, with Leonard Vanderhoop, Conrad or Conant Jeffers, Patrick Devine, Charles Grimes and Peter Johnson as crew. The boat left at 10:30 a.m. The men rowed out to the wreck and participated in further rescue efforts, saving thirteen people in conjunction with a revenue cutter that arrived on the scene.

The first lifeboat crew rescued seven survivors. *From left to right*: John P. Vanderhoop, Moses Cooper, James Cooper, Samuel Anthony, Samuel Haskins and Joseph Peters. *Courtesy of Eric Takakjian/Quest Marine Services and the Mariner's Museum, Newport News, Virginia.*

The second lifeboat crew worked with the revenue cutter *Samuel Dexter* to save seventeen men from the sunken ship. *From left to right*: Peter Johnson, Charles Grimes, Patrick Devine, Conrad Jeffers, Leonard Vanderhoop and James Mosher. *Courtesy of the Martha's Vineyard Museum.*

The Sinking of the *City of Columbus*

A fourth boat, owned by William James, was towed on wheels by an Ed Mayhew and Sons team of horses from Squibnocket, five miles away. It took an hour and a half to drag it to the shore, where it was eventually launched, at noon. The crew consisted of Edy Flanders as captain, with Cyrus Look, Ben Mayhew, Elliott Mayhew, William Mayhew and Seth Walker, all of Chilmark. By the time this boat was in the water, however, there were no more men to be rescued from the steamer. Asa Smith Esquire, keeper of the Massachusetts Humane Society lifesaving station at Squibnocket, reported this to C.B. Marchant Esquire, the society's district agent.

The efforts of the volunteers were exemplary throughout the harrowing ordeal. Of the two successful rescue efforts, the *Gazette* noted, "Never was a boat managed in such masterly manner in such adverse circumstances." And "too much cannot be said in praise of all these men who endangered their own lives to save the sufferers." A man from nearby Noman's Land, F.A. Noble, offered effusive praise as well, speaking of the "highest terms of the efficiency of the lifeboat, and the skillful manner in which it was handled."

The Massachusetts Humane Society had organized the Wampanoags as volunteers. The Humane Society, a precursor to the U.S. Coast Guard, supplied lifeboats and recruited volunteers. The society was state-supported, supplemented by public contributions. Members of the society had strategically positioned some fifty-seven lifeboats along the Massachusetts coast, as well as three more on inland waters. Men were recognized and rewarded by the Humane Society for their rescue efforts.

A key man in the rescue effort was Samuel Anthony (1860–1928), who described the efforts of the Wampanoags to rescue survivors of the *City of Columbus*. Anthony was interviewed by editor Samuel Keniston of the *Vineyard Gazette*: "He also indicated very clearly how the boat was held up to within a safe distance of the wreck by the oarsmen and steersman, while intelligent direction was given to the survivors in rigging to jump, one at a time, whenever a sea receded from the ship."[45]

Later, Anthony submitted an article to a publication called *Along the Coast*, which appeared in 1909, twenty-five years after the shipwreck.[46] *Along the Coast* printed accounts of the day-to-day operations of the surf men of the Life Saving Service. Anthony's dramatic tale of the rescue effort resonated a quarter century after the event.[47]

The following excerpts are taken from Mr. Anthony's account of the rescue:

> *The wreck of the* City of Columbus *on the Devil's Bridge of Gay Head, Mass., took place when the moon was nearly at its full, but one of*

those nights when the clouds are very heavy and the wind blowing a stiff gale from the west southwest, and the land on both sides of Vineyard Sound was covered with snow.

Samuel Anthony recalled how the event began:

I was told that there was a steamer on the "bridge" and that volunteers were wanted to man the lifeboat, so I hurried on my clothes and started to the scene…it was quite a hard task as the boat house was on a high bluff, but we finally succeeded and just as the sun was coming up, we launched the lifeboat. The high sea drove us back on the beach and we had to jump overboard to save our boat from being smashed to splinters on the rocks.

[Getting the boat afloat again,] we were on our trip to save lives or lose our own in trying. Our captain was A. Peters. We all took off our boots and were in our stockings, so our wet feet would not freeze…we made very slow headway against the fearful gale. It was a sight that was ever to be remembered by the ones who witnessed it. There were men in the rigging and on the pilot house, and some on the main stays and they were drenched through with the waves that would break over them.

He continued, "We finally got our grappling fast to the wreck and dropped just clear of the wreckage and tried to plan for saving the lives of the poor fellows in the rigging…we called for them to jump, one at a time."

Anthony witnessed the men drop from the rigging:

One by one they jumped and we saved them, and never lost one. As fast as we hauled them into our boat we took off our coats and wrapped around their shoulders.

When we were getting the ones that we saved, the pilot house began to give way…as the bow of the steamer was not under water, as she had run on a large rock.

While we were at the wreck, the men on shore were not idle for they had seen the life raft with what had appeared to them to be five men clinging to it some distance out in the Sound. The other Massachusetts Humane Society lifeboat had not got to the shore at the time from Squibnocket, so some of the men launched an old seine boat but owing to the gale and sea they did not get through the surf and the boat was smashed to kindling wood and some of the men nearly drowned. All of the men on the raft were lost.

The Sinking of the *City of Columbus*

All the men on the life raft were crew members of the *City of Columbus*: Archibald Morrison, Edwin Fuller, Gus Harding, William Murray, William Fitzpatrick and Richard Sullivan. The next day, it was reported that the empty raft drifted ashore at Cedar Tree Neck, along the Vineyard shore, some ten miles from the wreck.[48] As Anthony reported, no one survived on the life raft:

> *We got back to shore about one o'clock and landed at the wharf. The men on shore hauled us up out of the life boat by a rope. We were all very much cramped up but soon got limbered up. The boat then went back after another load and a new captain and crew, but the revenue cutter boat was coming through the Sound headed for the wreck so that they put them on board of her and helped to save twenty-one. I got a silver medal for the work that I did and prize it more than any of my personal belongings.*

Anthony later became a member of the Gay Head Life Saving Service, a precursor to the United States Coast Guard.

The aforementioned revenue cutter was the *Samuel Dexter*, which operated under the auspices of the federal Treasury Department. Revenue cutters provided an armed, maritime law enforcement operation that patrolled the waters in search of smugglers or captains who had not fulfilled their tariff responsibilities. Revenue cutters also provided rescue services to ships in distress, so the *Dexter* was a welcome sight to those stranded on the *City of Columbus*. The *Dexter* provided encouragement and assistance to the Wampanoags, who alone had provided all the rescue efforts.

The *Dexter* was 143 feet long, half the size of the *City of Columbus*, but with an able crew of forty capable of aggressive rescue efforts. The ship was built in 1874 and named for Samuel Dexter (1761–1816), an attorney who served in the administrations of presidents John Adams and Thomas Jefferson. Dexter was apparently neither well known nor well respected, as the Coast Guard notes that "his temperament and intellectual endowment ill suited him for that minute diligence and attention to intricate details which the departments of War and Finance imposed on the incumbents of office." However, his namesake, the ship, handled details with precision.

The revenue cutter *Samuel Dexter* happened upon the wreck of the *City of Columbus* and assisted in the rescue efforts of passengers and crew from the shrouds, in conjunction with Wampanoags in the Humane Society boat. *Courtesy of the United States Coast Guard.*

The wooden-hulled schooner *Dexter* was equipped with a steam engine and two mounted guns, manned by a crew of seven officers and thirty-three enlisted men. The ship served in the U.S. Revenue Marine (USRM) Service from 1874 to 1908. Coast Guard files on the *Dexter* state, "She patrolled the Long Island Sound and east to Nantucket, enforcing customs laws, patrolling regattas, and assisting mariners in distress." The *Dexter* [49] also patrolled from Edgartown to the Nantucket Shoals and off Gay Head. Thus, it was not unusual for it to be in Vineyard Sound in the late morning, as it was on January 18.

When the crew of the *Dexter* spotted the *City of Columbus* in distress, unlike the *Glaucus*, which had passed on by at daybreak, Captain Eric Gabrielson immediately steamed up to assess and assist in the rescue operations already underway by the Humane Society. (The captain of the *Dexter* established a Martha's Vineyard connection when he married an Edgartown woman, Mary Isabella Wimpenny, in 1867.)

Because of gale-force winds and detritus from the wreck strewn in the waters, the *Dexter* had to remain at a safe distance. Able coordination between the Wampanoags in the second run of the Humane Society boat, captained by James Mosley, and the crew of the *Dexter* allowed the offloading of survivors who had been picked up by the Wampanoags. The Wampanoags made three trips to the *Dexter*, transferring five, six and then two survivors for a total of thirteen men.

The grim accounts of the wreck in the national press were countered by descriptions of the dramatic rescue: "It was seven long hours before any succor reached them."[50] The first trip by the Humane Society arrived before 10:00 a.m. and rescued seven survivors. "Two hours later the revenue-cutter *Dexter*, Captain Eric Gabrielson, approached and a second lifeboat was sent out from Gay Head. The boats from the cutter brought away twenty-one, of whom four were dead before they reached the cutter." Lieutenant John Rhodes, USRM, said of the Gay Head boats: "The crew did noble work, their boats were handled with skill."[51]

It was evident that the public hungered for positive news to offset the horrors of the wreck. Indeed, accounts of the rescue assumed poetic proportions. "And here occurred one of those heroic actions which light up the prosaic peaceful revenue service as with the gleam of battle," claimed the *Harper's* account of the rescue effort. Details were presumably gleaned from an interview with Lieutenant Rhodes himself, who was at turns modest and self-promoting in recounting his exploits as he coordinated the *Dexter*'s rescue efforts from a lifeboat in the water.

Harper's reported:

> *Leaving his own boat, and boarding the lifeboat, Lieutenant John Rhodes tied a line about himself when about thirty feet from the wreck, and sprang into the sea. Before he reached the wreck, a spar struck him, and he sank. Drawn back into the boat, he insisted on a second attempt, and this time succeeded in bringing back the last man in the rigging. The poor wretch was hanging head down, his feet caught in the ropes, and begged, "For God's sake, do not touch me!" He breathed his last before the cutter was reached.*

The *City of Columbus* shipwreck and rescue operations were captured in a sketch published in *Harper's Weekly* on February 2, 1884. This hand-colored lithograph was done by Charles Graham from a sketch by Gustav Crane, an officer on the revenue cutter *Dexter. Courtesy of James Claflin, LighthouseAntiques.net, Worcester, Massachusetts.*

This episode earned Lieutenant Rhodes congressional recognition and presidential promotion and ensured his fame among the bravest participants in the rescue effort. (The man who died in the rescue attempt was Caleb Richardson, whose wife had drowned earlier.)

A few years after the incident, Alfred Pairpoint interviewed Captain Gabrielson of the *Dexter.* Gabrielson described how Lieutenant Rhodes and other officers "plunged into the seething waters several times and rescued all the lives they could, in which humane work they were ably assisted by the Gay Head Indians in their staunch whaleboats, on that bitter disastrous morning."[52] Captain Wright was the last man to leave the ship, at 3:30 p.m., after twelve hours aloft. He could not swim.

Lieutenant John Rhodes was born in 1850 and lived with his mother in Madison, Connecticut, when he was not at sea. He was promoted to the rank of second lieutenant in 1880, four years before his historic rescue effort. According to the *New York Times,* "For his gallantry on the occasion of that disaster, he was advanced by the President [Chester Alan Arthur] to the position of First Lieutenant." Rhodes later spent several years with the Marine Revenue Service along the coast of Alaska. In one incident, he intercepted thousands of dollars of smuggled opium. Rhodes died in 1890 at the age of forty.

After Lieutenant Rhodes was in the water, he was hit by a spar and returned to the *Dexter*. A second second lieutenant, Charles Kennedy, commanded a lifeboat and rescued four more men, whom he brought back to the *Dexter*. For this, he was awarded a silver medal.[53]

Dorothy Scoville described the rescue efforts in her account of shipwrecks off Martha's Vineyard:

> *As the Gay Head boat transferred those rescued, a boat from the* Dexter, *in charge of 2ⁿᵈ Lt. John Rhodes, went out to the wreck. Six more half frozen men were picked from the masts, now precariously swaying with every reaching wave. On a second trip one more man was brought to safety. Lt. Charles D. Kennedy with new men, then temporarily replaced Lt. Rhodes and his exhausted crew. Three more survivors were rescued, including Captain Wright.*[54]

Once the last man was taken off the rigging, the *Dexter* steamed back to New Bedford with survivors. It arrived at 7:00 p.m. on Friday, January 18, bringing the first news of the disaster.

The story of the rescue efforts was tarnished slightly over the years by a couple of disgruntled crew members of the *Samuel Dexter* who sought attention for their role in the rescue efforts and belittled their lieutenant, John Rhodes, for his valiant behavior.

It was not until the autumn of 1927, forty-three years later, that two members of Rhodes's rescue boat shared their perspective, filled with resentment at the accolades awarded to Rhodes. (To allow so much time to pass before telling their side of the story is unusual, although they claimed they tried to get a hearing earlier.)

In their account of the rescue effort,[55] Captain Josiah Pease and seaman Manuel Silva, members of the *Dexter's* crew, played a large part in the rescue effort. Pease was coxswain of the lifeboat. They affirm most of the facts of the story, adding details such as "coaling the ship in Edgartown" and noting that the *Dexter* had patrolled Block Island prior to coming upon the *City of Columbus*.

The 1927 piece quotes Silva describing Rhodes as "thoroughly incompetent and more than half-drunk" and claiming that he rescued no one but himself. Pease, also of Edgartown, confirmed Silva's comments. The article offered little corroboration beyond suggesting that Rhodes wanted to bring the lifeboat on the windward side of the wreck rather than the lee. Also, Rhodes was offered a shot of rum after the mishap with the spar; Pease and Silva were denied even a cup of coffee. An added point is that Silva used an oar to steer when the boat's rudder broke; that was admirable but is a common means to maneuver a small boat.

In short, the 1927 piece has the ring of rivalry and angst at not getting attention for their rescue efforts.

Word quickly reached Vineyard Haven of the wreck off Gay Head. At 11:30 a.m. on January 18, the collector of customs dispatched Lieutenant D.G. McRitchie of the *Speedwell* to Gay Head to assist in the rescue effort. "The tug got underway at once. McRitchie soon began to encounter wreckage. He passed several floating bodies and then met a lifeboat riding almost submerged in the tug's path."[56] Huddled in the lifeboat was passenger Sherrington Vance. The *Speedwell* rescued Vance and then continued on to provide assistance to the *Dexter* and the remaining crew of the Humane Society. The *Speedwell* returned to Vineyard Haven at 8:30 p.m.; along the way, it "picked up three bodies, four trunks, a box and an overcoat."

While the rescue was underway, at least one seaman with an artistic bent sketched the scene of the final hours of the *City of Columbus*. The sketch was promoted in the national press and gave added credence to the shipwreck as news of the drama spread across the wire services.

At the end of the day on January 18, 1884, eleven survivors of the wreck were alive, safely ashore on Martha's Vineyard. No one on the mainland was aware that anyone had been rescued at Gay Head. Seven men had been rescued by the Wampanoags in the first lifeboat effort, and four more had made their way ashore in a lifeboat. (The twelfth survivor, Captain Vance, was pulled from a lifeboat of the wrecked steamer and deposited in Vineyard Haven.) Seventeen survivors were aboard the revenue cutter *Dexter* when it docked in New Bedford that Friday evening.

The Sinking of the *City of Columbus*

In Gay Head, the survivors were housed by the Wampanoags and lighthouse keeper Horatio Pease. It was not until Sunday, January 20, when the tug *Nellie* arrived at Gay Head with reporters and family members that the survivors were "found." Reporters were amazed that the eleven survivors were remarkably well recovered from the wreck. But many bodies of deceased passengers were housed in huts on the shore.

Four men paddled a lifeboat ashore:
James Brown, passenger
Simon Gallant, seaman
Roderick McDonald, quartermaster
Thomas O'Leary, fireman
(Charles James, passenger, expired on the shore)

Seven men were rescued in the first lifeboat:
Thomas Butler, fireman
Henry Collins, assistant engineer
John Hines, fireman
Michael Kennedy, seaman
Edward O'Brien, seaman
William Spaulding, purser of Boston (at the house of Horatio Pease, keeper)
Fred Tibbetts, passenger

Crew of the first Humane Society boat:
Joseph Peters
Samuel Haskins
Samuel Anthony
James Cooper, twenty-one (James was the last survivor of the rescue crew; he died in 1945 at the age of eighty-two)
Moses Cooper, eighteen (James's younger brother)
John P. Vanderhoop.

Crew of the second Humane Society boat:
James Mosher
Leonard Vanderhoop
Conrad (or Conant or Thomas) Jeffers
Patrick Devine
Charles Grimes
Peter Johnson

9
The News

Historian William Quinn, a shipwreck expert, offers a word of caution regarding research of nautical events:

> *You must be careful when quoting from published sources as reporters tended to embellish here and there to enhance their stories. Crew members who relate details are wont to protect themselves and many times lie through their teeth so they will not be blamed for any accidental actions on their part.*

With that admonition, Mr. Quinn suggests, "If you read the same information from different sources, it is usually somewhat reliable." He concludes, "There is a definite need for correct information where shipwrecks are the subject of essays and books."

Word of the wreck of the *City of Columbus* first reached the mainland in New Bedford, along the Massachusetts south shore, in the early evening hours of Friday, January 18, when the revenue cutter *Samuel Dexter* docked in the harbor. This was a major news story. The *Dexter* arrived in New Bedford at 7:00 p.m. bearing the few surviving passengers and crew and several bodies of the deceased. "The news she brought quickly spread over the city and indeed over the country, creating widespread horror at such an awful catastrophe, and universal sympathy for its victims."[57]

As Captain Wright emerged from the *Dexter*, "his face wore a careworn look which was truly pitiable and the expression of his eyes told of the trouble which weighed upon his spirits."[58] He immediately telegraphed Alfred Nickerson at the Boston and Savannah Steamship Company in

The Sinking of the *City of Columbus*

Boston. Nickerson, in turn, booked a special train on the Old Colony Line, which left Boston at 3:30 a.m., arriving in New Bedford ninety minutes later.

Survivors of the wreck were offloaded from the *Dexter*, stunned by the calamity they had undergone, some unable to comprehend the magnitude of the experience. Many of the survivors boarded the special train back up to Boston to try to put their lives back together.

When the train pulled into Boston at 8:45 a.m., more than five hundred anxious people were there to greet the survivors and learn about the tragedy. As reported from Boston, "Fifteen survivors of the wrecked steamer *City of Columbus* arrived this morning on a special train from New Bedford, many of them in a pitiable condition and some too dazed to render intelligent accounts of the wreck."[59] The Farnsworth boys "report they saw one boat containing seven women upset near the wreck and the sea soon demolished it."

Meanwhile, Zephaniah Pease, of the *New Bedford Morning Mercury*, gathered details of the disaster, prepared a story for his newspaper and passed on the news to the *Boston Globe*; it was then picked up by the Associated Press. It was the *Morning Mercury* story, written by Zephaniah Pease, that contained the first word of the rescue efforts by the Wampanoags of the Humane Society and the *Samuel Dexter*.

(The *New Bedford Morning Mercury* was a prominent weekly newspaper established in 1807. Zephaniah Pease began his career as a reporter at the *Mercury* in 1880, replacing Nathaniel Morton when the latter moved on to the *Boston Globe*. Pease became editor of the *Mercury* in 1894 and later published his definitive work, the *History of New Bedford*, in 1918. The *Mercury* ceased publication during the Great Depression in 1929.)

Newspapers around the country recognized that this dramatic disaster was a major news event, and the story was quickly reprinted nationwide. Newspapers had garnered stories off the wire service for years and reprinted them virtually verbatim. With the Associated Press (AP) wire service, news flowed across the country with amazing speed.

Formed in 1846 by a quintet of New York newspapers, the AP was designed to share expenses associated with gathering and transmitting news via a not-for-profit cooperative. The remoteness of battles in the Mexican War and challenges of reporting news from pony express to boat and telegraph made the AP a sensible alternative to multiple reporters struggling to gain access to a story.

In John Brown's raid at Harper's Ferry in 1859, and through major battles of the Civil War, the public was informed of events quickly and in depth

This illustration was featured in *Frank Leslie's Illustrated News* on February 2, 1884. It offers a graphic view of the rescue efforts by the Wampanoags in the lifeboat to the right and the *Dexter* to the left, with detritus from the sunken ship. The lower sketch is a view from the shore, with the wrecked steamer and dead bodies washed up along the beach. *Sketches are credited to William Frizzell. Courtesy of the Martha's Vineyard Museum; photograph by Paul Cournoyer.*

by AP reporters. The wreck of the *City of Columbus* occurred shortly after the attempted assassination of President James Garfield in 1881, which was national news. Newspapers successfully managed to provide comprehensive and timely reports of major events of the era.

News organizations expanded exponentially in the latter half of the nineteenth century. Western settlements created the need to gather news for a public hungry to learn of events in other parts of the country. The Associated Press made it possible for an efficient dissemination of current news nationwide. And by the 1870s, a primitive teleprinter transmitted text over telegraph wires, so newspapers could have a story ready to print right off the telegraph lines.

It was not always an easy time for the Associated Press. Shortly after the shipwreck, an AP reporter interviewed Captain Andrew Burnham of the Board of Inspectors of Steam Vessels. Burnham told the reporter that the captain of the *Glaucus* had admitted, privately, that he recognized the *City of Columbus*, saw the signs of distress but did not stop because "the Captain did not wish to be delayed on his trip." Burnham found this most heartless.

The next day, Burnham denied that he had spoken with the AP reporter. Nevertheless, the reporter insisted that such a statement had been made.

Because the story of the wreck of the *City of Columbus* was national news, the impact was shared across the country. The *New York Times*, in its Sunday edition on January 20, with a dateline of Savannah, reported, "News of the wreck of the *City of Columbus* and the terrible loss of life was received with profound sorrow in the city. There were no residents of Savannah aboard. Deep sympathy is expressed for the calamity, which has carried sorrow to many families in New England." But business must go on. The *Times* reported that "the *City of Macon* will take the place of the wrecked *City of Columbus* on the Boston line." Actually, the *Gate City* replaced the wrecked *City of Columbus*.

The *Times-Picayune* of New Orleans, also on January 20, reported on "the loss of the favorite Atlantic Coaster Steamer." The *Las Vegas Daily Gazette* of the same day posted headlines: "No Child or Woman Saved" and expounded how "it was fearful the way the women were swept away." The *Arkansas Gazette* reported, "A dispatch from Wood's Hole states that Captain Wright has become violently insane." Reports on the loss of life, personal suffering and helplessness of the passengers stirred the national conscience.

And there was immediate reaction in national editorials describing the disaster, assigning blame and giving credence to a search for the cause of the wreck. It could not be blamed on bad weather or mechanical difficulty; this disaster was man-made. In Cincinnati, the *Tribune* reported, "The Treasury Department has decided to make a very thorough investigation into the loss of the *City of Columbus*. The steamboat inspectors of that district will be directed to convene a Court immediately."[60]

The *Vineyard Gazette*, the local weekly publication of Martha's Vineyard, published its first report and commentary on the wreck a week after the catastrophe. By that time, the story had made headlines across the country, and editors devoured the stark story and repeated its gruesome details.

Editor/proprietor Samuel Kenison acknowledged the immediacy and locality of the crisis and its impact on the Vineyard:

The disaster of last Friday has stirred our Island community to a degree seldom experienced in respect of tragedies, however harrowing, in which the people had no personal interest. But this horror occurred at our very doors, its victims and survivors—some of them—found temporary resting place within our borders, and every distressing circumstance and detail has been brought home with a sharpness of realization which never attaches to occurrences more remote.[61]

This illustration, featured in the *Daily Graphic*, vividly imagined the travails of the passengers in the sinking of the *City of Columbus*, with dozens of helpless people washed off the deck of the ship. *Courtesy of the Martha's Vineyard Museum; photograph by Paul Cournoyer.*

In a sidebar, Kenison justified his copious columns on the wreck: "We have devoted considerable space to an account of the shipwreck this week for the reason that it belongs somewhat to the history of this locality."

The *Gazette* obliquely observed that "the *Boston Herald*, in its issue of Saturday, contained a sweeping arraignment of Light-keeper Pease and the inhabitants of Gay Head, and on Monday took it all back, with ample apology."

Harper's Weekly, a prominent national publication, took two weeks to assess the disaster, but then the editorial staff did not mince words: "The wreck of the *City of Columbus* shocked the country as no like disaster has in years. It was so sudden, so complete, so terrible, and, we must add, so cruelly causeless, that the whole community felt a sense of personal grief and indignation over the accounts of it."[62]

Of the wreck, *Harper's* reported that "the scene as one of terrible confusion." Then the article focused on the question being asked from New York to San Francisco:

> *That a sound and seaworthy vessel on a comparatively clear night, with the chief landmarks distinctly visible by which its course was to be guided, should have met with such sudden and swift disaster, and that not one in five of those on board should have been saved, is not to be explained by any of the inevitable risks which those must face who go down to the sea in ships.*

In short, how could this tragedy have happened?

And the final casualty: "the hundred precious human lives drowned or beaten out by the wild waves that swept the sunken but well-known reefs were lost by the acts of men, intelligent and accountable, with ample means for safely performing the trust they had assumed." This interpretation in *Harper's* captured the horror of human error and the disastrous consequences of inattentive navigation and sought to quantify the wreck for a sense of closure. It was difficult to do.

A second national publication, *Scientific American*, viewed the disaster as an opportunity to improve maritime safety. *Scientific American* had praised the impressive launch of the *City of Columbus* in 1878; now it assumed the role of a scolding senior statesman, searching for the means to save helpless passengers aboard a sinking ship. The piece opened with: "Every little while some terrible calamity on the ocean deeply stirs the public mind, and awakens the apprehension of all who 'go down to the sea in ships.'"[63]

That so many people drowned was a catastrophe, yet the ship was properly stocked with required lifeboats, a life raft and sufficient life preservers: "The life saving appliances were abundant and of approved kind, but the circumstances were such, on a rough coast in a high sea, that they were of comparatively little use, most of those saved having been rescued by help from outside the ship." The author looked for an innovative rescue device.

The article proposed an improved technique for ocean rescues. It noted the difficulties in lowering lifeboats, "and when a vessel has struck and has a heavy list, as in the case of the *City of Columbus*, the boats on the lower side become useless, while it is doubly hard to launch those which are on the side out of water."

Scientific American offered a challenge to develop a "life saving appliance which needs no preparation; which is always in full working order; which will float its occupants high out of water; which can be got clear of a stranded or foundering vessel without swamping or staving." That goal was admirable, but as the author admitted, "it is a difficult problem to solve, no doubt, but there ought to be enough inventive genius in this country to solve it."

From a provocative lifesaving challenge to the depths of gruesome exploitation, the national press devoured details of the wreck and then regurgitated aspects in detail.

Scandal sheets focused on dramatic elements, such as how passengers donned life preservers only to be washed overboard and drowned. Artists rendered full-page illustrations to capture tawdry aspects of the tale.

And the words of the stories reiterated the sense of doom:

> *The water filled the state rooms and cabin slowly, and there was the continual pounding of the vessel on the ledge, but the full extent of the danger was not realized. Within twenty minutes, however, all below decks became untenable, and then the real horrors began.*[64]

A popular tabloid of the era was *Frank Leslie's Illustrated News*, a literary and news magazine in vogue during the latter half of the nineteenth century that featured patriotic or dramatic news stories with eye-catching covers. *Leslie's* was founded in 1852 and published weekly, on Tuesdays. Frank Leslie died in 1880; his widow, Miriam Florence Leslie, a suffragette, succeeded him as editor. It ceased publication in 1922.

According to *Leslie's*, the *City of Columbus* "had passed the most dangerous point in the channel, and was wrecked on what is usually considered the least dangerous ledge." Then, *Leslie's* attacked the crew for its response to the disaster: "Still another [lifeboat] was manned by a few officers and men, and went off without a passenger." And it offered a salacious view of the disaster: "During the forenoon the bodies of two young women floated up below decks and drifted away."[65]

Of the forty men who clung to the rigging, "one by one they succumbed to the cold, until only a score were left, when, after eleven weary hours, the life boat was able to take them off."

A dramatic visual, captured on the cover of another tabloid, the *Police Gazette*, indicated that as many as sixty people were washed off the deck by a single wave.

The *Daily Graphic* was among the first newspapers to offer numerous illustrations. The *Graphic* was a New York publication, founded in 1873, by a group of Canadian engravers. It continued as an "illustrated evening newspaper" until 1889. The *Daily Graphic* glorified news events and embellished stories to attract readers with its dramatic drawings.

The country was captivated by the calamity. Besides the press, ministers rose in their pulpits to ponder the disaster. There had not been a death toll of such magnitude since the Civil War, and this was so unexpected, so pointless and so heart wrenching.

On the second Sunday after the wreck, January 27, Reverend Wright Butler of New Bedford preached on a theme of "fidelity until past the point of peril." He asked, "Who is responsible, and what is the reason for the wreck and disaster of the *City of Columbus*?"

THE DAILY GRAPHIC

VOL. XXXIII.   NEW YORK, FRIDAY, JANUARY 25, 1884.   NO. 104.

THE STORY OF THE CITY OF COLUMBUS.
IS THERE NO CHIVALRY LEFT?—WHY IS IT THAT ONLY MEN ARE SAVED?

The cover of the *Daily Graphic*, a week after the wreck, featured gruesome deaths of women and children. Use of a dramatic front page illustration helped sell newspapers, just as today's tabloids, prominently placed in supermarket checkout aisles, draw attention. *Courtesy of the Martha's Vineyard Museum; photograph by Paul Cournoyer.*

Pointedly, he assigned blame: "The responsibility for the loss of the *City of Columbus*, in its widest apportionment, is limited to four men: the Captain, the second mate [Harding], the quartermaster and the lookout." The preacher said the lookout only notes objects he sees; the quartermaster is an automaton, almost mechanical in his assignment. The second mate began his watch less than two hours before the disaster and still seven miles from the wreck, so he had ample time to rectify the course. The minister saved ultimate blame for the captain. Although Wright was "a brave, true, tried man," with ninety-one voyages over thirty-one years at sea, the minister condemned Captain Wright "for leaving the deck of the *City of Columbus* before all dangerous points were entirely passed."

Reverend Butler concluded by expounding on our responsibilities toward others:

> *But let us never forget that however humble and inconspicuous our status, there is none so poor of us that we do not keep inward some other's happiness, that it is in our negligence or vigilance to imperil or secure that which to these self-interested ones is dearer than life.*

One man's carelessness impacts those around us; we are our brothers' keepers.

Another minister, Reverend Thomas King of New York, preached on "The Divine Providence in Its Bearing on the Wreck of the Steamer *City of Columbus*." He noted that "no disaster, within recent years, has been more appalling." He spoke to the infinite freedom of God but added that man has limited, or finite, freedom. God allowed this to happen. Man, with his finite freedom, failed to prevent the disaster. The minister concluded, "It is a consolation to know that those who have been removed to the spiritual world through this disaster may come in spirit to the loved ones left behind." Those who died may reappear as angels to family and friends.

Words from the pulpit were aimed at calming the angst of the public and granting abiding peace. Across New England, funeral services were held, with comforting remarks offered to the families of the deceased. Public accounts of the wreck were designed to memorialize the victims and bring closure to the disaster.

It was noted on the Vineyard that no mention of the wreck was made in local services because no resident of Martha's Vineyard had succumbed in the tragedy.

Seven years after the disaster, Alfred Pairpoint referred to the "lamentable shipwreck," "the doomed steamer," and waxed poetic as he described the *City of Columbus*, "steered to her destruction on the reef, in sight of the lighthouse off Gay Head."[66] Pairpoint commemorated the shipwreck as an event that "shook the community of Eastern New England and elsewhere with feelings of dismay, sorrow, and bereavement."[67]

As to the cause, Pairpoint offered an otherworldly speculation: "Those in responsible authority must have been dazed, bewitched, bewildered." He spelled out the nautical opportunities: "When they deliberately, on a moonlit night, steered the doomed vessel and its living, human freight to instant destruction, as if those in command of the ill-fated steamer were lured on to the rocks by some wicked sirens of the deep." The implication that the crew was in the sway of a witch casts the story in a spectral light.

The Sinking of the *City of Columbus*

Through the years, authors, researchers and maritime historians have viewed the wreck of the *City of Columbus* as a tragedy of epic proportions. For generations, books have described the horrors of the wreck. An eminent scholar labeled it "one of the most terrible marine disasters in the annals of Massachusetts steamship navigation."[68] Another noted that Captain Wright "steer[ing] too close to the Vineyard after rounding West Chop was the consensus of some."[69] A third author referred to the "reef of rocks" and the "most disastrous shipwreck of the century."[70] And William Quinn wrote, "The steamer made an error in dead reckoning and came to grief on Devil's Bridge."[71]

Robert Farson wrote that "one of the most unnecessary sea tragedies in New England took place on a bitterly cold night in January, 1884."[72]

The travesty of the shipwreck of the *City of Columbus* has resonated through the years as one of the more senseless disasters along the New England coast. It is inexplicable that a luxury steamship, on a routine trip with more than 100 people aboard, should be so far off course. But twenty-five years later, in 1912, the world watched as the "unsinkable" *Titanic*, a luxury leviathan, collided with an iceberg buried in the deep, and 1,500 people lost their lives.

The shipwreck of the *City of Columbus* was a major news story when it occurred in 1884, and the horror of the tragedy still echoes more than a century later. Whether assessed by the tabloid press of the late 1800s or thoughtful maritime histories decades later, the root cause of the disaster still elicits shudders when people learn of the helplessness of the passengers, especially the women and children, who drowned in the calamity on Devil's Bridge.

10

The Bodies

That 103 people died in the wreck of the *City of Columbus* was a travesty. When the ship began to sink, women and children were washed off the deck into the freezing waters and died of hypothermia, drowning or being struck by detritus from the wreck itself. Many bodies were never recovered.

High seas and strong winds continued following the shipwreck, which precluded further rescue operations. In the first hours and days after the wreck, no one on the mainland was even aware that anyone had been rescued and harbored in Gay Head.

Local reportage described the challenge of rescue operations: "A heavy south west wind was blowing all the morning...Tonight, a terrible gale is blowing across the Sound and vast quantities of wreckage are coming ashore in Falmouth."[73] It was, after all, the middle of winter, and gale-force winds thundered across the sound.

Eventually, the winds died, the skies cleared, the seas calmed and searchers could walk the shoreline of the Vineyard to recover corpses. On the Elizabeth Islands of Cuttyhunk and Nashawena, locals patrolled as well, although the current washed most bodies and wreckage toward Vineyard beaches.

It was reported that "frozen corpses are slowly being picked up and identified at different points along the wild and dreary coast."[74] Bodies washed up along the western shores of the Vineyard, at Clay Wharf in Chilmark and Gray's Landing and Lambert's Cove in West Tisbury, some fourteen miles from the wreck. There was a report of two bodies "picked up on the back part of Edgartown."[75]

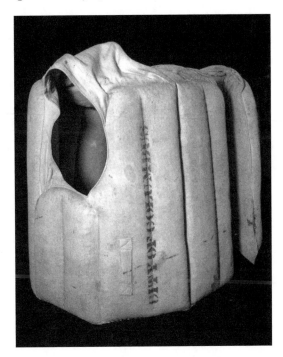

Sufficient life preservers were aboard ship; most victims died from hypothermia. This cork preserver was manufactured by the Kahnweiler Company of New York, "Builder's [*sic*] of Metallic Life Boats and Life Rafts." West Tisbury's Mabelle Medowski recalls the preserver. "It was up in the attic for a while." She says, "I think my mother [Sarah Reynolds Luce] wanted it to go to the Museum." The Luce family lived on Indian Hill, near where wreckage washed ashore. *Courtesy of the Martha's Vineyard Museum.*

The remains were often naked, encrusted with sand or tangled with seaweed and shrouded in ice. It was observed that "most of the bodies were mutilated in a greater or less degree, and their clothing was filled with sand." Ironically, many recovered bodies were buoyed by life jackets, although the person died in the freezing waters.

One body was found in the harbor of Menemsha Bight. Another woman's body was found in West Chop. Her frozen corpse, loaded on a wagon, was drawn along an icy roadway into Vineyard Haven.

Among the saddest scenes was recovery of the body of a youngster, described by the Dukes County medical examiner Dr. Leach, as "a small boy, a handsome little fellow, who proved to be Coburn Mitchell, also found in the harbor" of Vineyard Haven. That was a long way for a body to drift from the wreck. His body was "clad only in a night-shirt."

A distant descendant of the family of Coburn Mitchell furnishes background that encompasses the Atkinson, Belyea and Merrill relationship, all of whom died in the shipwreck:

> *Robert Bayard Belyea was an ancestral uncle. Our ancestral grandfather was Louis Bulyea of Saintonge, France, who came to New Amsterdam* [New York] *in the late 1600s. They settled in Tarrytown and were active members of the Old Dutch Reformed Church in Sleepy Hollow, New York. Louis's descendents lived in that area until the Revolution, at which time they moved en masse (as Loyalists, of course) from Tarrytown to New Brunswick, Canada.*
>
> *Robert married his half first cousin Elizabeth Belyea. Robert and Elizabeth had three daughters and one son. Alice Maude Mary (called Mary) married Atkinson and had a son, Wilmot. Mary's sister Antoinette Louise married Ivan Merrill. They had a son, Richard Coburn Merrill. On Christmas Eve 1883: three weeks before the wreck, Alice Maude Mary's husband died.*
>
> *I suppose the recent deaths of said family members prompted Robert to take his daughter Mary, her son Wilmot and the other grandson, Richard Coburn Merrill, on vacation in January 1884. The plan was to sail from Boston to Savannah. Of course, they never made it. Of the five Belyea family members who died—and they all died—I believe that three were never found, including Robert and wife Elizabeth and one grandson. Alice Maude Mary and I think it was her nephew Richard Coburn were brought ashore. They were dead. I understand some family members retrieved the remains and took them away for burial. I know not where.*[76]

The body of Lillie Small, mother of two-year-old Darius, was recovered. A pair of baby's shoes was found frozen to her dress.

The task of determining the identity of the victims took place in Capawock Hall in Vineyard Haven. Identification was supervised by H.H. Smith. John Holmes worked as a clerk under the medical examiner, Dr. Leach. It was a gruesome, emotionally draining assignment.

This elaborate memorial in Beaufort, South Carolina, marks the grave of Lillie Small, mother of Darius Small Jr., both victims of the shipwreck. Wording on the memorial reads, "In memory of Lillie wife of Capt. D K Small aged 23 yrs 5 mos 2 dys lost with her child on the *City of Columbus* in Martha's Vineyard Sound, Jan'y 18, 1884 but her body was found and conveyed to this resting place. Though lost to sight to mem'ry dear." Of her son, the memorial reads, "He carries the lamb in his bosom." The two-year-old's body was never found. *Courtesy of Maureen Keillor; photograph by Joyce Dresser.*

The *Gazette* observed that "a deep gloom seemed to settle over the village as the dead bodies of those who were washed ashore, or picked up by small crafts, were, one after another, brought to Capawock Hall for identification." Many bodies were not immediately identified, and others simply never surfaced.

Three unidentified bodies were described:

#13: male, 5'6", 155 lbs., good black suit, Congress boots
#17: female, 135 lbs., only black lisle stocking and heels
#18: male, 5'10", black hair, heavy mustache and black suit with new boots

While his body was not recovered, it was reported that Cornelius O'Leary, alias "Black Port," had worked as a fireman at the Cocheco Print Works. His pocketbook was picked up. "It is supposed that O'Leary shipped as fireman on the *City of Columbus* and was lost."[77]

Bodies of shipwreck victims that washed ashore in Gay Head were housed in huts by the shore until they could be transported to Vineyard Haven and on to Boston for identification and interment. *Courtesy of the Martha's Vineyard Museum.*

The grisly task of recovery and identification was made more depressing by the wintry weather. "The feeling of horror and gloom which has prevailed along the Massachusetts coast has been intensified by lowering clouds and storms."[78]

One of the first rescue efforts was conducted by the steamer *Storm King*, chartered by the Boston and Savannah Steamship Company, owners of the *City of Columbus*. The crew of the *Storm King* searched all along Vineyard Sound and managed to pick up nine bodies along the coast, as well as four survivors, the ones who made landfall in Chilmark. Dead bodies, as well as survivors, were transported to New Bedford and thence to Boston.

A second steamer, the *Monohansett*, plucked ten corpses from Vineyard Sound and transported them to Vineyard Haven, where they were identified and forwarded on to Boston by train. (The *Monohansett* had served as dispatch headquarters for General Grant during the final months of the Civil War and then resumed ferry service on the Vineyard.)

Three bodies were hauled out of Vineyard Haven Harbor by the USS *Speedwell*. While crew members aboard these rescue boats had the best intentions, sometimes the lure of lucre was too tempting. The commander of the *Speedwell*, M. Ritchie, "ordered the arrest of two of the crew of the vessel this morning on suspicion of stealing a gold watch from the body of one of the Gay Head victims which was picked up by the *Speedwell*."[79]

A week after the wreck, five tugboats still searched the waters off Gay Head.

The United States steamer *Verbena* took soundings to determine if the buoy that marked the Devil's Bridge was set too near the shore. It was thought perhaps it had been incorrectly set or had drifted from the ledge. The *Verbena* was sent out to dispel the rumor that the buoy had been carelessly set or allowed to drift.

The *Storm King* from New Bedford continued to patrol Vineyard waters.

A boat from Woods Hole, the *Confidence*, was chartered by the family of the Turkish consul (Iasigi) lost in the wreck. This private vessel searched for the missing man without success.

Thomas Scott, the well-known diver from New London, arrived with his tugboat *Alert*. New York underwriters, who had insured the *City of Columbus*, requested that Scott assess the damaged steamer. In 1884, Wrecker Scott conducted twenty-three assessments of shipwrecks off the New England and New York coast. His career spanned twenty-three years, from 1879 to 1902. Most of the two hundred wrecks he examined were schooners, according to research by Jamin Wells (*Ships on the Shore*), but he did conduct surveys of some twenty-three steamers, including the *City of Columbus*.

The *Hunt*, from New Bedford, was utilized by Boston diver John Olsen.

Across Buzzard's Bay, in New Bedford, the steamers unloaded recovered remains. The atmosphere in the city manifested a sense of loss and awe; businesses all across the city slowed as people awaited news of lost family members or friends who had been aboard ship.

Recovered bodies were offloaded either in New Bedford or Vineyard Haven before being shipped up to Boston. An announcement in New Bedford alerted family and friends that the bodies deposited by the steamers would remain in New Bedford until the train took them to Boston.

In New Bedford, "there was an overwhelming sadness to that ghastly scene and almost no conversation."[80] The sorrow of identification of these helpless victims taxed authorities. Family members were distraught. The *Monohansett* and the *Storm King* were both used to transport the deceased from Vineyard Haven to Boston: "The shipping of the bodies from Vineyard Haven to Boston was a cruel disappointment to persons who had come to the city [New Bedford] to identify friends and the action was bitterly commented upon."[81]

Years after the disaster, an account of professional peers was reported in the press. Zephaniah Pease assisted in the search for bodies and filed his report:

> *Pease had obtained his job on the* Mercury *when Nathaniel J. Morton, rising in his profession, went on to the* Boston Globe. *Now young Pease, on the deck of the tugboat Nellie, identified the body of his predecessor. Friends read bravery into the story that human flotsam told. Morton was fully dressed, cravat, muffler, carefully buttoned coat. Friends said he must have met death as he faced life, ready in his profession for any emergency.*[82]

Reports of more bodies surfaced. Evidence indicated that bodies remained within the hull of the sunken steamer. Wrecking master Captain Baker was said to "believe that the bodies on the port side of the wrecked vessel are in their state rooms and that the state rooms are in intact."[83]

The report continued:

> *Captain Baker argues that the* City of Columbus *was not sunk by the water which filled her forward compartments when she struck, but by the waves which broke over her deck when she rolled over on her port side. These waves submerged the cabins on the port side and probably drowned the occupants in their berths.*

Efforts were underway to locate bodies still trapped in the steamer.

A month later, three men from Gay Head explored the wreck "and fished out of the steerage the body of a female child about 18 months old. It was in perfect condition. The body is at Vineyard Haven."[84] This was the last body recovered.

The Sinking of the *City of Columbus*

The following tale bears retelling.[85] It was recorded by a man named William A. Gill, who sailed as a mate on the five-masted ship the *Governor Ames* of Portland, Maine.

"The following day came in with light south west wind, so we got underway." The fellow telling the story was at the windlass, hoisting his ship's anchor off Gay Head, and caught sight of a sparkle on the anchor chain. It was "a gold oval tie fastener that you could fasten your necktie to your shirt front." The ship's captain suggested that the clasp came from a passenger of the steamer *City of Columbus*.

The wreck of the *City of Columbus* was caused by "misjudgment in the wheel house," according to Gill's anecdote. "The captain did not take into consideration the heavy current and tides, and the *City of Columbus* piled up on Devil's Back Ledge to the west of Gay Head, and soon was breaking up."

Most of the passengers were in their staterooms, with doors locked, when the ship went down, according to this story. Wreckers were sent from Boston to salvage the ship.

The first diver to go down was from East Boston.

This diver was often away from home. His young wife grew lonely. Sometimes she would go to the movies, visit friends or go dancing.

> *The diver left home after bidding his young wife goodbye, saying just he was not sure how long he would be away on the wrecking job as the ship had a full cargo, and they were going to recover some of it...He knew the job he had to do to break open the staterooms and take out the bodies and send them up to the wrecking tug which was waiting for them on the surface.*

The diver prepared for his salvage operation. His assistant fastened his helmet and checked his air hose and lifeline. The diver's thoughts

> *went back to his home and his young wife, wondering what she was doing and everything was well with her, dropping off from the ladder on the side of the tug and in a few minutes he was down on the main deck of the wreck, as divers wear heavy, lead weights around his waist and on his shoes, and can descend very quickly to many fathoms deep. As it was a very bright, sunny day overhead, the sunlight penetrated the water down so the diver could see very well around the deck.*

Now the story assumes another dimension:

> *The first stateroom he came to he put his pinch bar at the side of the door and quickly forced it open. As he did, two bodies came floating past, a young man and a young woman. They sank to the deck at his feet. He stooped over the woman and dropped her quickly. He recognized his own wife he had left at East Boston a few days ago, before the* City of Columbus *was wrecked.*

Immediately, this diver "came back up in a hurry. As soon as he got on deck of the wrecking tug, he stripped off all his diving gear and asked to be sent home to Boston, as he was through with diving and would not ever put on a diving suit again." He never spoke to anyone of what he had seen "but kept to himself, wondering, just wondering. Could this be possible, his beautiful, young wife he had left just a short time ago. So happy and contented in their nice home, and they had planned on their first wedding anniversary in just a month."

Back home he found a letter from his wife. She explained she had met a friend at a dance and fallen in love. They planned to run away where she could never be found. She emptied their bank account and booked passage on the steamer *City of Columbus* bound for Savannah, Georgia. "From there, they would go west. She closed the letter wishing him love, and goodbye." The story concludes, "Such was the yarn of the *City of Columbus* and the heartbroken diver, which was true."

Whether there is any veracity to this cautionary tale, it does evoke vivid images.

11
The Retrieval

T he *Vineyard Gazette* referred to the shipwreck as the "Gay Head horror"
and termed the event an "occurrence at our very doors."

Besides the 29 passengers and crew rescued by the Humane Society, 103
bodies had to be located, retrieved and transported to Vineyard Haven or
New Bedford and on to Boston for identification, notification of next of kin
and burial. Once survivors had been rescued and bodies recovered, efforts
got underway to salvage baggage, freight and furnishings that floated from
the sunken vessel.

The *City of Columbus* was filled, too, with a quantity of freight, for the F.W.
Nickerson Company, now the Boston and Savannah Steamship Company,
had been established initially as a commercial line to transport manufactured
material south in exchange for agricultural products headed north.

The bulk of products headed south consisted of shoes and boots produced
in the mills of the Merrimack Valley and shipped for distribution and sale
along the coastal plains of Georgia and Florida. In the cargo hold on the
City of Columbus's last trip were barrels of rum, cases of shoes and boots, tubs
of butter, shipments of baked beans and salted codfish, as well as a carriage
boxed for shipment.

On the Vineyard, much of this cargo washed ashore:

> *Up on the Island beaches, the sea tossed its loot. Though the* Columbus
> *sailed light, in her hold were 237 cases of shoes, five half barrels
> of New England rum, 200 packages of bacon, four cases of baked
> beans, 25 nests of tubs and other miscellany. Islanders salvaged tubs*

of butter, scraped it off and found good food beneath the spoilage. They accumulated washtubs by the dozen, cases of shoes, useful, shattered furniture and furnishings.[86]

In addition, wooden planks from the decking of the ship soon served as firewood.

It was reported that one hundred men walked along the north shore of the Vineyard, picking up articles from the wreck such as trunks, boxes of shoes, mattresses and the capstan (cylinder to hoist the anchor) of the steamer. The *Gazette* advertised "Found and Picked Up" items as Vineyarders sought to return items they recovered. The Boston and Savannah Steamship Company had no interest in damaged cargo, as insurance monies covered losses. Personal items washed ashore such as trunks, bags and cases. Most of it was of little value but did offer curious Vineyarders a peek at the passengers' personal baggage.

One classified ad, entitled "Picked Up in Vineyard Sound," described a large quantity of shoes and other articles found on the north shore of the Vineyard. The ad was signed "E. Athearn, No. Tisbury and W.T. Norton, No. Tisbury." When no one claimed the items, they were appropriated by locals.

William Manter of Chilmark found furniture, blinds and boxes of shoes near Roaring Brook, "which the owners can have by proving property and paying charges." Found or picked-up notices continued for a few weeks and detailed a quantity of shoes and other artifacts. Two boxes of shoes turned up on the south beach.

Remarks in the Chilmark town column included "Articles from the wrecked steamer continue to wash ashore. Several boxes of shoes were picked up last week." Curiosity-seekers made the trek up island to view remains of the wreck. The bell of the steamer,[87] trunks, boxes of shoes and a chest of tools owned by James Brown of Lawrence, the carpenter bound for Savannah, washed ashore.

Even today, artifacts surface in various situations or disappear as time smothers memories of the disaster. At the Aquinah Cultural Center, formerly the Edwin Vanderhoop Homestead, Tom Manning or Leonard Vanderhoop constructed a cabinet from planks that washed ashore from the *City of Columbus*. It is in the kitchen of the center. Beverly Wright recalls that it has three shelves, and her parents used to store newspapers underneath; she played in the cabinet as a little girl.

The great chandelier that illuminated the stairway that linked the Social Hall and the main saloon washed ashore and was retrieved by one

Scavengers gathered along the shore below the Gay Head cliffs to retrieve artifacts of value or curiosity from the wreck. Cases of shoes were the most common find. *Courtesy of the Martha's Vineyard Museum.*

of the rescuers. Anne Vanderhoop of Aquinnah remembers the light that brightened the Harrison Vanderhoop Homestead off State Road:

> *Harrison took me in there. He showed me this lamp that came off the* City of Columbus. *It was an oil lamp. He said he had it made into an electric lamp. It was quite decorative. A beautiful antique. It's attached to the ceiling, like a chandelier. Hope they didn't throw it out. It was bronze and it took Harrison some time to do it. His father brought it home. He was one of the rescuers of the* City of Columbus.

Unfortunately, the Vanderhoop Homestead was sold and demolished; the new owners did not know the history of the chandelier. It may have been salvaged, again, but we could not locate it.

Other artifacts include candles from the ship. At least two Vineyarders claim to have them. Chairs, a door, a cushion and crockery have been taken from the sea. And at least one deadeye has once more seen the light of day. (A deadeye is a disc with a grooved edge. Lanyards, or lines, run through a deadeye to steady shrouds or rigging that secure the mast of a ship.)

Shortly after the wreck, James Mosher came upon a trunk with papers worth $25,000. He delivered it to the owner, and the *Gazette* observed, "The best of care is taken of whatever of value lands, and it is either advertised or sent directly to its owners." Two detectives dispatched to locate passenger trunks found them and returned to Boston.

Besides merchandise that washed ashore, the vessel itself was an object of interest. Salvage operators sought to raise the sunken ship. "The wreck of the *City of Columbus* lies firmly planted on the sunken ledge, with her bow and masts above water, and there she may stay for weeks. It is not likely that any attempt will be made to raise the hull."[88] The newspaper story added there was a "great hole in her starboard side, through which the tide pours like a torrent." Fragments of jagged rock lay on the sandy bottom nearby.

> *A diver went down this morning on the port side of the wreck and found the damage more serious than was at first reported, several large rocks having been apparently moved by the steamer striking them. The diver proposes to visit the interior of the wreck as soon as the weather permits.*[89]

Wrecker Thomas Scott was on the scene. Scott was a flamboyant figure. "If pluck, ingenuity and mechanical appliance can float the ill-fated steamer, Captain Tom is the man for the work, and if he says it can't be done, the man that makes the attempt had better try to whistle down a gale of wind."[90]

Salvage efforts were underway soon after the shipwreck. Wrecker Tom Scott appropriated the anchor, the safe and the ship's compass, as well as much of the rigging. The stern of the hull was raised by the Boston Towboat Company. *Photograph courtesy of Chris Baer.*

At first, the weather was too difficult to conduct a successful dive. "The sea was roaring and surging within the confines of the wreck in a fearful manner, and the billows occasionally rose against the deck upon which the reporter stood."[91]

As the *Vineyard Gazette* reported, Scott, standing on the deck, "was caught on the crest of an immense breaker and hurled into the air and overboard." Days later, the *Times* reported, "Scott was able to remain two hours under water and complete the survey."[92]

Scott completed his initial survey of the hull for the marine underwriters. He reported a three-foot-square hole, twenty feet from the stern of the vessel. Also, he identified smaller holes and cracks along the hull. Portions of the smokestack, machinery, lines, sails and wreckage were strewn along the ocean floor.

Wrecker Scott continued his salvage operation. "Scott visited her [*City of Columbus*] on Saturday, took away the anchors, parts of the rigging and other articles of value."[93] And he was not averse to appropriating souvenirs. "The golden sign that once ornamented the stern of the ill-fated *City of Columbus* is now nailed over the door of one of the Wrecker Scott's workshops in New London."[94] He located the ship's safe,[95] "and the ship's compass was found in the sluiceway carved by the ship, twenty feet from the stern."[96]

Scott believed the ship had struck the rock known as the Back of Devil's Bridge, and drifted backward, carving a furrow in the sandy ocean floor. The main forward section was in adequate condition, but a mass of debris surrounded the ship's stern. In Scott's professional opinion, the ship had suffered too much damage to attempt to raise it.

News that recovery, as well as salvage operations, was suspended was confirmed.[97]

> It has been concluded to abandon all further efforts to recover any property from the wreck of the City of Columbus. The tide runs with such velocity where the wreck lies that the vessel is rapidly going to pieces. Nothing of value has been recovered. There is no hope of the recovery of any bodies, as it is supposed the decks have been washed away and the hull is open to the action of the waves. The next storm of any severity will probably obliterate all traces of the steamer.[98]

John Olsen, the diver who gave this assessment, believed it best to leave the vessel as is.

Months later, the stern of the hull was raised by the Boston Towboat Company. "A gang of divers and bargemen" did the job, working "with steam hoisting apparatus, being securely anchored directly over the sunken hull."[99] The intent was to remove the boilers, engines and machinery for reuse. "Some portions of her cargo are still in her, notably many cases of pork and barrels of potatoes," the article concluded.

Life on the Vineyard returned to normal. The Baptist Society sewing circle was held, the Literary Union met and a church social was well attended. The Good Cheer Club gathered in West Tisbury, with reading, music and refreshments. Edgartown selectmen announced that the bridge over Sengekontacket Pond was considered "unsafe for public travel, and the same has been closed until further notice." Nearly one hundred pounds of coffee was found by workers at the Sengekontacket Bridge; it may have washed up from the *City of Columbus*.

In national news, in late January it was reported that Frederick Douglass married a second time, to a white woman, a copyist in his office. And Jefferson Davis was failing; his eyes gave him trouble and his step was feeble.

12
The Awards

The *Gazette* commended those brave islanders who responded to the request for help and rose to the occasion. The second issue after the wreck glorified the rescuers: "Too much cannot be said in praise of all these men who endangered their own lives to save the sufferers."[100] This theme followed the tragedy of the wreck: Vineyarders needed to find a positive aspect to counter the disaster. The Wampanoag Humane Society crew became instant heroes.

It was suggested that the community should be praised, as well as the boatmen. In an editorial, the *Gazette* opined that "on no portion of all our coast could greater heroism have been shown in the rescue of the living. Nowhere could more becoming conduct have been manifested in the treatment of the dead."

Insurance adjuster Captain G.W. Mudgett of Edgartown, a marine underwriter's agent, was quoted as saying that "the behavior of the Gay Head people in all the respects named was admirable in the extreme."

The brave men who risked their lives were seen as heroes of the tragedy. Instead of dwelling on the women and children who drowned and the passengers and crew who succumbed to the violent waves and wind, Vineyarders honored the Native Americans who saved a few souls from disaster.

The Massachusetts Humane Society was cognizant of the heroic efforts of the Wampanoag crews. Native Americans would be recognized for their efforts. Funds were allocated. Certificates were designed. Medals were minted.

The Humane Society voted to make awards "to persons engaged in rescuing or attempting to rescue the survivors of the wreck of the *City of Columbus.*"[101] It was determined that the twelve men of the first and second boats would each receive a silver medal and twenty-five dollars. They rescued those who dangled from the ship's shrouds for hours.

The money had a major impact on the Wampanoag volunteers; $25 then was equivalent to $600 in present value. Money in the hands of hardworking men was important, especially as it was an acknowledgement of their bravery.

In many ways, the medals were appreciated more than the money. It meant recognition for the bravery the Wampanoags had exhibited in the rescue efforts. It was affirmation by the white man of the courage of the Native Americans. Even today, more than a century after the presentation of awards, descendants of the Humane Society crew honor the memory of these brave souls and treasure the official recognition.

Jane Slater of Chilmark writes, "My great-grandfather's brother, James T. Mosher of Chilmark, was the captain of the second lifeboat out and back to the *City of Columbus*. He didn't bring home any artifacts, but he was awarded

The Samuel Anthony medal is one of several awards still extant. Anthony considered it his most prized possession. The wording reads: "For gallant and successful efforts in saving twenty of the passengers and crew of the Steamer *City of Columbus* off Gay Head Jan. 18 1884." These medals were presented to the Wampanoag rescuers by the Massachusetts Humane Society. *Property of Beverly Wright; photograph by Joyce Dresser.*

a medal that ended up with his niece, Lucy Vincent." She donated his silver medal to the Martha's Vineyard Museum in 1967.

Beverly Wright still has the silver medal earned and treasured by her great-grandfather Samuel Anthony. It was his most prized possession. Other extant medals include those of James F. Cooper (silver) and Benjamin Mayhew (bronze), housed in the Martha's Vineyard Museum archives, and that of Lieutenant Charles Kennedy (silver), with Richard Boonisar of Cape Cod.

Mark Anthony DeWolfe Howe (1864–1960), editor and author, compiled an exhaustive history of the Massachusetts Humane Society. He described the *City of Columbus* as the "most disastrous wreck that has happened for very many years on the Massachusetts coast."[102]

Of the rescue effort, Howe wrote, "The inhabitants quickly responded, and the boat was manned, without delay, by a volunteer crew." It was not an easy task. The Humane Society boat "was rowed out with great difficulty in the heavy sea, her crew being so exhausted on getting to the wreck, that they were unable at first to do more than catch hold of the steamer's flag halyards, streaming from the gaff, and hold on to recover their strength."

So much wreckage was strewn in the waters that the Humane Society crew could not approach the wreck. Men in the rigging "had to jump into the sea and trust to swimming or to friendly waves to get near enough to the life-boat to be taken aboard."

Howe confirmed that the crew, on the second trip, worked in conjunction with the revenue cutter *Dexter*. The Wampanoags made three trips to the revenue cutter. Altogether, Humane Society volunteers saved twenty of the twenty-nine men who were rescued.

The Humane Society distributed awards on February 15, 1884. The *Vineyard Gazette* praised the heroes in an article entitled "Honor to Whom Honor is Due." More than one hundred residents from various Native American settlements across the Vineyard assembled in Gay Head. The general inspector of the society's lifesaving stations presented the awards.

Silver medals were awarded to those who risked their lives to save another person's. Each of the twelve men in the Humane Society boat received twenty-five dollars and a silver medal. The men who manned the Squibnocket boat, although too late to save anyone, each received a bronze medal and fifteen dollars.

The men in the whaleboat, smashed on the rocky shore and unable to offer aid, each received ten dollars. That crew consisted of Thomas and Henry Jeffers, John Lula, Charles Stevens and Simeon Devine. The latter earned an additional ten dollars for carrying news of the wreck to Squibnocket with the need to get the second lifeboat. Zaccheus Cooper received five dollars for use of his horse to deliver the news.

The lifeboat housed in Squibnocket, dragged out to Gay Head, was launched too late to rescue anyone. Nevertheless, each of the crew still received bronze medals and fifteen dollars. These six men risked their lives. Edy Flanders (captain), Cyrus Look, Ben Mayhew, Elliott Mayhew, William Mayhew and Seth Walker made up the crew. William James, owner of the boat, received sixty dollars for his boat.

Horatio Pease, lighthouse keeper, received a certificate and twenty-five dollars. Frederick Orian Poole was also honored with a certificate and fifteen dollars. Poole was the assistant light keeper who first noticed the wreck and alerted Horatio Pease.

Zaccheus Cooper, James Thompson, Aaron Cooper, Horatio N. Pease, Thomas Jeffers and Charles Lyon each received $5 for "caring for rescued persons in their houses." The people who brought hot drinks and "restoratives" to the beach were recognized for their humane attentions and exertions in caring for the survivors. Each was awarded $5 and a certificate. (In 1884, $5 was the equivalent of $120 today.)

The crew of the *Dexter* received $200 to be divided among themselves.

This photograph bears the images, and names, of the Wampanoag Humane Society rescue teams. *From left to right:* John Vanderhoop, Reverend A.P. Sheilds, Simon Devine, Patrick Devine, Charles Stevens, Tom Manning, Leonard Vanderhoop, Jim Cooper, Sam Haskins, Sam Anthony, Frederick O. Poole, Tom Cooper, James Mosher and Joe Peters. *Courtesy of Beverly Wright; photograph by Joyce Dresser.*

The awards made a big impression on the little community. The Humane Society volunteers were local heroes.[103]

Following the Humane Society presentation, the assembled throng was invited to witness the demonstration of a new lifesaving device. The Hunt gun was designed to save people from a grounded sailing ship. The gun was a small cannon that housed a shot line aimed to fire over a ship, and the line would latch on to the rigging. Passengers would then mount a sling, or a breeches buoy harness, and slide down the line to safety. (This contraption would not have worked with the *City of Columbus*, as the steamer was more than a quarter mile offshore, well beyond the distance of the gun. For ships grounded closer to shore, however, it had some appeal.)[104]

A second public presentation enjoyed even more adulation.[105] This assemblage occurred on February 26, eleven days after the first ceremony, and consisted of donations collected by newspapers to reward the rescuers. Seventy-five people gathered at Gay Head and another thirteen in Squibnocket for a total of eighty-eight participants.

Cornelius B. Marchant, customs collector and member of the Boston Press Gay Head Fund, coordinated distribution of $3,500, raised by newspaper readers. Again, each member of the two crews was recognized, and this time each received $160, which would be comparable to $3,800 today. Imagine what that money meant to the residents of Gay Head in the late 1800s. After the monetary awards were presented, Marchant asked if anyone else needed compensation. "There was a general rush for the rostrum," reported the *Gazette*. Marchant asked the audience to be seated. When he again asked if anyone had been omitted from payment, "the whole remaining assemblage rose as one man."

Everyone, it seemed, felt they had assisted, supported, contributed or participated in the rescue effort. Marchant doled out the remaining funds, and people were most appreciative. Sixteen people received ten dollars and nineteen got five dollars. The monetary awards were "received with the liveliest manifestations of gratitude." The *Gazette* noted, "The Indian nature is not over demonstrative, but the awards for the most part appeared to be thankfully received, and will certainly be of great assistance." At the end of the day, Marchant had distributed a total of $3,005 in Gay Head and an additional $495 to people in Squibnocket.

Other rewards were given to Lieutenants Rhodes and Kennedy and the crew of the *Dexter*, including an impressive testimonial certificate presented by the City of Newport, Rhode Island.[106] The State of Connecticut recognized Lieutenant Rhodes for his "gallant conduct." Rhodes's rank was raised by President Chester Alan Arthur. Lieutenant Warrington Roath of the *Dexter* was also recognized.

A letter from Congressman John Long was published in the *Gazette*. It was in response to B.T. Hillman, Chilmark town moderator. Hillman had sought congressional acknowledgment of the Gay Head Indians. Congressman Long concurred, writing that "the Gay Head men deserve most handsomely. Never was there a nobler exhibition of humanity and courage."

A resolution was filed in the Forty-eighth Congress by Congressman Long,[107] commending the officers and crew of the *Dexter* and "the men who manned the lifeboats from shore." *Harper's* lauded the Native Americans, noting that "the thanks of Congress were unanimously voted to the men of the life-boats."[108]

Coast Guard records report that the first Congress, in 1790, authorized ten federal ships to prevent smuggling and enforce federal tariff and trade regulations. This was known as the Revenue Cutter Service, of which the *Samuel Dexter* was a part.

The Humane Society of the Commonwealth of Massachusetts notes that "in 1785, a group of Boston citizens met several times at the 'Bunch of Grapes' tavern to consider the formation of an organization modeled on the British Royal Humane Society." The goal was to eliminate senseless deaths associated with shipwrecks.[109]

The Humane Society promoted "an awards system with a financial stipend for those who risked their lives to save others." The society established huts and lifeboats along the Massachusetts shoreline. The first hut, stocked with supplies for shipwreck survivors, was situated on Scituate Beach in 1787. The first lifeboat for volunteers on shore to rescue people in

The Massachusetts Humane Society was formed in 1785. Besides enlisting volunteers, the society provided lifeboats and survival huts along the coastline in the event of a shipwreck. *Courtesy of the Martha's Vineyard Museum; photograph by Joyce Dresser.*

a wrecked boat was housed in Cohasset in 1807. Medals and money proved to be incentives for volunteers. The work of the Humane Society served as a model for the United States Life Saving Service and eventually the United States Coast Guard.

The United States Life Saving Service (USLSS) was created in 1871. Like the Humane Society, it was made up of volunteers who received medals as a reward for their rescue efforts. For many years, the USLSS and the Humane Society competed in rescue efforts. The benefit of this combined effort was that, during a mighty storm, more people would be saved through joint efforts.

The USLSS merged with the Revenue Cutter Service in 1915 to form the United States Coast Guard, again under an act of Congress. Thus, a single maritime service was created, dedicated to saving lives at sea and enforcing the nation's maritime laws.

The Humane Society continued to station lifeboats and lifesaving stations along the Massachusetts coast into the 1930s. The last of its equipment was taken out of service in 1946. Since then, according to Humane Society records, "a cooperative relationship between the Coast Guard and The Humane Society was established in 2002 in a Memorandum of Understanding, affirming the shared history of the two institutions and their commitment to improving safety on the waters."

One member of the United States Coast Guard has sought posthumous recognition for the Wampanoags who rescued passengers and crew from the *City of Columbus*. Chief Boatswainsmate Lonnie Clark has made a concerted effort to seek lifesaving medals for the volunteers. "There's nothing that prevents you from getting a life-saving medal," he says. Mr. Clark has contacted members of Congress, as well as the Coast Guard, in his effort to obtain twelve posthumous awards for the Humane Society volunteers.

The Coast Guard's response has been that the Humane Society honored these men in 1884, which is true. Mr. Clark feels the men are still entitled to recognition by the Coast Guard. "These men more than deserve it," says Mr. Clark.

13
The Inquiry

Three consecutive activities got underway after the shipwreck. A concerted effort was made to retrieve and identify bodies. The Humane Society rewarded the rescuers. And the public demanded to know the cause of the wreck.

An editorial in the *New York Times* questioned how such a disaster could have occurred:

> The loss of the City of Columbus *should be made the subject of a thorough investigation. She went ashore on a night when there was no fog, and Gay's Head light* [sic] *was so distinctly visible that the officer of the deck had no excuse for not knowing precisely where the vessel was.* [The ship was] *wrecked either by gross ignorance or the gross carelessness of the officer in charge of the deck.*[110]

The *Times* claimed it was akin to the Staten Island Ferry crashing into a lighthouse in broad daylight.

Steamship inspectors Chairman Andrew Burnham and colleague Andrew Savage launched an investigation into the cause. Their review was intended to begin on Wednesday, January 30, 1884, but was postponed due to the illness of Captain Wright. Wright was devastated by the disaster, but within a week, he managed to present himself before the inquiry.

The first meeting, therefore, convened at 10:00 a.m. on February 5, 1884. The *Morning Mercury* reported, "But long before that hour the interest in the inquiry was manifested by the large number of persons eager to obtain seats in the auditorium." The intent of the investigation was to assign blame for the wreck of the *City of Columbus*.[111]

Captain Wright was the primary subject of the investigation, and his response to questions dominated the inquiry, even when others testified. Wright was adamant that he had given the correct course to his second mate, that southwest by west would have cleared the Devil's Bridge by two miles. His revised course of west-southwest, ordered as the ship passed Tarpaulin Cove, would have brought the *City of Columbus* more than three miles west of Gay Head.

Wright confirmed that he had retired to his stateroom as the *City of Columbus* traversed Vineyard Sound. He sat on the floor, with his back to the heater and his head in his hands, adjacent to the pilothouse, within feet of the wheelman, McDonald. Although he was supposed to take the starboard watch, he assigned it to Second Mate Gus Harding, who was twenty-one and not a licensed pilot.

The captain defended his offering assistance to passengers with life preservers: "I have to look after my passengers and crew." As to why lifeboats were not successfully launched, Wright responded that "the water ran in so sudden it took everybody by surprise, and they didn't have time to do it." He stated that shortly after the ship struck and listed to port, water burst through the hatches. "I think the water came into the saloons, and washed away her after hatch and poured down into her after compartment." Sea water was shoulder deep in the saloon.

The second witness was Second Assistant Engineer Henry Collins, who also described hatches bursting open from incoming water. Bulkheads were supposed to be watertight but had been left ajar. Collins remarked that with the ship listing dangerously to port, its rails were under water, and great seas broke across the decks. He was unable to lower any lifeboats as the disaster was precipitous. Although Collins tried to board the life raft, it was washed out to sea before he could do so. He hoisted himself aloft in the rigging, instead, and was saved.

The next day of testimony, February 6, focused on Quartermaster Roderick McDonald, the man at the wheel. McDonald was thirty-five, with fifteen years of maritime experience. He displayed ignorance about the Savannah run, unclear about which lighthouses were along the route and what course he was given, and he said he thought the Gay Head light was closer than usual but didn't make much of it. Only when Second Mate Harding ordered him to "port the wheel" did McDonald realize he was off course.

("Port the wheel" means to turn the wheel to the left, which makes the ship turn right. The wheel is attached to the rudder, which turns the ship in the opposite direction.)

McDonald did not imply that Second Mate Harding was asleep on his shift, although he claimed the mate had a history of nodding off. He stated that Harding was not known to imbibe. The deceased Harding could not refute accusations. McDonald denied that he was asleep at the wheel.

Edward Leary, twenty-seven, testified that he was the bow watchman when the ship ran aground. He had been on duty less than two hours when the accident occurred. Like McDonald, he was ignorant about which lighthouses were along the coast. Leary stated he had never seen lifeboats lowered for a drill.

Next up was Edward O'Brien, forty, a seaman with five months of experience aboard the *City of Columbus*. He, too, had never been part of a lifeboat drill.

John White, seaman, noticed the buoy that marked Devil's Bridge but was ignorant of the ship being off course.

John Hines, fireman, testified that he felt the ship lurch to a stop and then grind on the rocks. He saw water coming through the hatch and hurried up on deck.

Thomas Butler, fireman, tried to lower a lifeboat, but a wave washed it away. He recalled a boat drill, but boats were not lowered.

The third day of testimony was held on Thursday, February 7, 1884. Thomas Leary, fireman, stated that he did not know to which lifeboat he was assigned.

William Spaulding, purser, had shipped aboard the *City of Columbus* with Captain Wright for the past sixteen months, since September 1882. He was in charge of both freight and passengers. "Ocean water was already in the Social Hall, which was one deck above the main saloon," said Spaulding. He alerted passengers of the disaster. As purser, Spaulding believed there were eighty-one paying passengers, as well as children or infants under four years of age. Tickets were not purchased for young children, so they did not appear on the passenger manifest.

Andrew Pitman, steward, supervised the dietary staff. It was his responsibility to provide liquor to passengers; crew members were denied liquor unless they were ill. Neither Wright nor Harding had imbibed, to Pitman's knowledge.

Pitman was awakened as the ship ran aground. He testified, "I stopped to put studs in my clean shirt when I heard Captain Wright cautioning the

This whistle cover and photograph from the *City of Columbus* are currently (2012) on display in an exhibit entitled "Ice and Isolation: The Islands in Winter in Cuttyhunk" at the Cuttyhunk Historical Society. The society also has extensive coverage of the wreck, reprised in the *Falmouth Enterprise*. *Courtesy of Cuttyhunk Historical Society, Kathryn Balistrieri and Roxy Leeson.*

passengers to keep cool. I helped a passenger put on a life preserver, and tried to help a woman disengage herself from a door, but could not."

Pitman was assigned to the life raft, but it was full by the time he reached the deck.

On February 8, day four of the inquiry, Captain Wright could not explain how the wreck occurred. "God only knows" and "You must ask a higher power" were his explanations for the disaster. The *Vineyard Gazette* opined, "Neither of [these] replies served to throw much light on the situation."[112] Wright sounded genuinely befuddled as to why the ship ended up on the rocks.

February 11, the fifth day of testimony, focused on First Assistant Engineer Hiram A. Phillips. He described orders to reverse engines and then progress forward. There was no intimation, he said, that the ship had been wildly steered. Phillips ran the engines forward until the engine room flooded. When he came up on deck, "things were in a bad state."

Captain Thomas Hammond, a passenger in a stateroom, testified that as the ship passed through Vineyard Sound, the ocean was illuminated by moonlight. He never heard an order to lower boats, but the lashings were cut, and some boats drifted out to sea. Neither the tide nor a "wholesome wind" would have had an impact on the course of the ship, he believed.

Fred Tibbetts had a stateroom aft. He mentioned that he thought wearing his life preserver could frighten fellow passengers. Roommate Frank May offered his knife to slash the lines of the lifeboats; in the confusion, May was washed overboard.

Furber Hanson, a waiter, testified that this was his first experience working on a ship. When the *City of Columbus* struck, Pitman told him to alert passengers in the forward saloon, which he did. He stated that ocean water poured in the port side and rose to the doors on the starboard side.

February 21 marked the sixth and final day of testimony. John Olsen, a diver, spoke of a half-ton rock, some six feet high and eight feet around, which had been split off by the impact of the steamer.

Captain Wright was recalled.

Inspector Savage asked the captain, "Then you have no way to account for the ship getting so far to southward, by compass variation or otherwise?"

Wright responded, "No, sir."

Savage then asked, "Isn't there such a thing as bad steering, yawing and trying to verify it, etc."

Wright answered, "Oh, yes, sir; bad steering is one of the worst things we have to contend with. But that ship steered easily and by steam."

Savage questioned whether Wright felt it was practical to have one man perform the duty of both mate and pilot. What happened when that man had to rest? Wright said that he never slept on the seventy-hour trip. He also stated that he was not in a position to make steamboat laws but considered the role of mate relatively easy aboard such a ship as the *City of Columbus*.

Referring to his orders, Captain Wright testified that he had specifically said to his second mate, Gus Harding, "When Tarpaulin Cove light bears north, go west-southwest." According to testimony, Second Mate Harding never gave that order, and the wheelman, McDonald, never heard that order. Because Captain Wright went to his room and did not communicate further with the wheelman or second mate, the ship continued off course, without a licensed pilot in charge.

This panel was retrieved from a cabin aboard ship. The author of *Disaster on Devil's Bridge*, George A. Hough Jr., labeled it: "Lost on Devil's Bridge on Martha's Vineyard. January 18, 1884 with 103 of 132 aboard." *Courtesy of George and Mary Lu Hough; photograph by Joyce Dresser.*

The inspectors concluded that once the ship ran aground, "the backing of the engine, under the circumstances of this case, we think was a fatal mistake." When Captain Wright reversed engines to dislodge from the underwater boulder, this brought the ship into deeper water, which caused it to sink.

Blame for the accident was assigned to faulty steering, with additional issues of wind and tide pushing the ship farther south, toward the shore. The question was raised, "Why was not this divergence noted by the pilot in charge?" Captain Wright could not give a satisfactory response; he was utterly heartbroken about the wreck. However, he stood by his second mate. "He spoke in the highest terms of Augustus Harding, his Second Mate…the Captain says Harding was one of the most capable young men he ever met."[113]

Testimony from diver Thomas Scott was taken and reported by New London inspectors and then added to the Boston district testimony. After his several dives to the wreck of the *City of Columbus*, Scott confirmed that the ship struck the boulder, not the ledge. When asked if it were practicable to raise the ship, he said it would not be feasible.

Captain Maynard Bearse of the *Glaucus* took the stand. He claimed he saw waves breaking over the steamship but no sign of life. His conduct was questioned. He said he focused his glass (telescope) on the wreck to no avail. He had never been reprimanded for a slow passage, he said, and would have stopped had he seen any survivors aboard ship. Two *Glaucus* crew members confirmed that they saw no sign of life aboard the wreck.

The report of the inspectors was completed on March 4, and results were submitted to the supervising inspector general in New York.

The inspectors addressed the issue of Captain Maynard Bearse of the *Glaucus*, who bypassed the wrecked *City of Columbus*. They found no reason to suspend or revoke Captain Bearse's license or that of any of his officers.

In their final report, the inspectors stated, "We are forced to the conclusion that Capt. S.E. Wright was the only legal pilot on duty at the time of the disaster" and that "he was not at his post of duty as pilot." Furthermore, "for illegally delegating the performance of the duties of the pilot to others not authorized, and for inattention to his duties as pilot, his license as master and pilot is hereby revoked."

Captain Wright lost his license.

The Board of Supervising Inspectors of Steam Vessels included its report on the cause of the wreck of the *City of Columbus* in its annual proceedings in Washington, D.C., in January 1885: "A thorough and searching investigation was made, which fixed the responsibility upon the pilot, who was also master of the ship, and his license was revoked for gross neglect of duty." (The United State Steamship Inspection Service today is the Merchant Vessel Inspection Service of the United States Coast Guard.)

Interestingly, in the National Archives, a United States Coast Guard Abstract of Wreck Reports, 1878–1885, entry #938, includes the *City of Columbus*. Curiously, besides listing 83 passengers (not 87), 44 crew (not 45) and 99 lives lost (not 103), the cause of the wreck is characterized as a gale rather than pilot error.

14
The Courts

Alfred Nickerson, president of the Boston and Savannah Steamship Company, filed a brief[114] in the United States District Court on February 18, 1884, to limit liability for damages associated with the loss of the *City of Columbus*. This brief was directed at anyone who sought action against the company.

The intent of limited liability was to curtail any action that had commenced, as well as deny others from initiating a suit, thus to "prevent a multiplicity of actions." The limit on liability was to retain the value of the ship and freight to the extent to which any liability of the owners could be assessed.

The Boston and Savannah Steamship Company denied that either negligence or incompetence should be assigned to the company. "The disaster was beyond their control," a newspaper story read,[115] and the company announced that all liability claims would be contested in the United States courts.

Court cases can drag on for years. The *City of Columbus* case was no exception. It culminated in a decision by the Supreme Court of the United States on April 22, 1889, five years after the wreck. It was entitled *Butler et al v. Boston and Savannah Steamship Company*, and the Supreme Court's decision is published as 130 US 527 9 S.Ct. 612, 32 L.Ed. 1017. The case evolved from the wreck of the *City of Columbus*, where "most of the passengers and cargo were lost."

Regardless of the effort to limit liability, lawsuits were filed on behalf of passengers in the wreck of the *City of Columbus*.

One victim of the disaster was Elizabeth Beach of Mansfield, Connecticut. John Haskell Butler was appointed administrator of her estate. His name heads the case, which was an effort to recover damages from the wreck.

Two passengers who survived the shipwreck joined forces to file a separate case against the Boston and Savannah Steamship Company. James Brown and Sherrington Vance survived yet claimed losses from the wreck.

The court issued a monition, or injunction, against further legal action on February 28, 1884. Anyone seeking damages for loss in the wreck must submit proof of claims prior to July 1, 1884. Public notice of this monition was to be filed in local newspapers. The court ordered that no more cases against the owner of the company could be filed under "the admiralty rules of the United States supreme court."

The Code of Maritime Admiralty established the right of limited liability over events that occur within the territory of a state in an effort to protect shipowners who risk their sailing ships on the high seas. The code was designed "for the encouragement of shipbuilding and the employment of ships in commerce, the owners shall not be liable beyond their interest in the ship and freight for the acts of the master or crew."

This concept was defined in maritime law and then incorporated into federal statute. Loss, in this case, was not to exceed the value the owner held in the vessel and its freight. Limitation of liability was key to the case.

It was determined that limited liability extends not only to property injury or loss but also to personal injuries and death. By including personal injuries, the court said, "the probable purpose was to put American ship-owners on an equality with foreign ship-owners in this regard."

In abiding by an 1871 act to improve security aboard steam-propelled vessels, it was stated that the ship should have been under the control of

The ship bore two quarter boards. This one is now preserved in the Martha's Vineyard Museum; the second was affixed to wrecker Tom Scott's salvage shed in New London and then surfaced at Mystic Seaport Museum. *Courtesy of the Martha's Vineyard Museum.*

a licensed pilot. The master or owner is liable for damages. The primary allegation in this case was that the second mate was in charge of the *City of Columbus* at the time of the wreck; that, said the company, was a decision for the captain to make.

Exceptions were filed stating the law did not apply to personal injuries and death, that insurance money should be paid to the court and that loss of life was grounds to recover additional monies. The company responded that such laws were within the grounds of limited liability.

The court found that limited liability extends to claims for personal injuries, and further suits against the owners would be stayed. Insurance monies are not part of the interest on a vessel.

On the steamship, everything was lost—to wit, "its machinery, tackle, apparel, and furniture," according to court documents.[116] The claim was that the libellant (Boston and Savannah Steamship Company) was "liable and responsible to pay to them the loss and damages arising as aforesaid." The company's response was that, as owner, its liability was limited. The company claimed that such liability should "in no event exceed the amount or value of the interest of the libellant, as owner, in said steamship and her freight then pending."

The estate of Elizabeth Beach filed claim, stating that the *City of Columbus* was a "coastwise seagoing steamship" and that the disaster was caused by "negligence of those employed by the steamship company"; the second mate, Augustus Harding, "was in charge of the ship, and was not a pilot on those waters" and "no pilot was on duty." The ship should have been under the control of a licensed pilot, according to the charges brought in the lawsuit.

The suit charged negligence and carelessness on the part of the owners and sought damages of $5,000 compensation for Elizabeth Beach, as she "suffered great mental and bodily pain upon the vessel." Furthermore, the loss of her clothing and baggage was $150, which should be reimbursed. And the appellants felt entitled to receive $50,000 from the United States government for Miss Beach's death.

The Beach estate stated that the company should have been "indemnified for the loss of the vessel." The appellants requested that the company pay insurance monies to the court. The company admitted that it had received insurance money but had applied it to the vendors and mortgagees of the ship.

Butler, administrator of the Beach estate, retorted that under federal rules, the owner of the company "is liable for all loss and damage caused by the stranding of said steamship *City of Columbus*." In response, the company denied the allegation about the unlicensed second mate and stated that the captain was indeed in charge of the ship at the time of the wreck.

The case of James Brown was graphic. Brown spent three hours in a lifeboat with a passenger (Charles James) who "died from cold or exhaustion or fright." Brown, temporarily blinded and unconscious, was "dragged to the shore, and out from the surf." He was then treated at Massachusetts General Hospital in Boston for frostbitten toes and fingers. He claimed his

For decades, this cushion sat in a rear pew of the Lambert's Cove Church. Mabelle Medowski, ninety-two, recalls, "It came off the *City of Columbus*. My great aunt was living on the Island and she said it washed up along the shore. The cushion was not in my family. It had always been on the back seat of the church." *Courtesy of the Martha's Vineyard Museum; photograph by Joyce Dresser.*

"health is permanently impaired." Brown was accustomed to earning $2.50 per day; because he was incapacitated, he claimed damages of $25,000.[117]

The cases of passengers Beach and Brown were joined on April 10, 1885, and moved through the legal system as one.

A timeline of the subsequent four years includes the following:

1882: The Ocean Steamship Company, original owner of the *City of Columbus*, held the mortgage on the ship until ownership was transferred, in 1882, to the Boston and Savannah Steamship Company.

1885: The Ocean Steamship Company reported that "the loss of the *City of Columbus*, of the Boston and Savannah Steamship Company, matured the mortgage and insurance policies held by us in security for the notes given in payment for her purchase by that company. The insurance upon her has been collected and the unpaid balance on the notes liquidated."[118] Thus, the mortgage of the *City of Columbus* was effectively paid off by insurance.

1886: The Boston Towboat Company bought the remains of the wreck for $600.

1887: Ownership of the Boston and Savannah Steamship Company reverted to the Ocean Steamship Company, which continued operations until World War II.

Elements of the travails of passengers and their estates shed light on the plight of those who sought justice in the case.

We do not know if the following affidavit relates to the court case against the Steamship Company or another case. We know no more about the intent or result of this affidavit, although it may relate to inheritance. It was submitted by a friend of William Lapham, who was a passenger aboard the *City of Columbus* with his two young children. It speaks to the graphic ordeal of the tragedy:

> *Adelaide I. Burdon of Boston on oath depose and say that I was well acquainted with William A. Lapham. Having known William for ten years. He was a temperate man did not use spirituous liquors. He was drowned with his two children at the wreck of the* Columbus *at Gay Head. January 18th 1884. On the afternoon of January 17th 1884 I went with him to the steamer* Columbus *and saw him take passage and sail on said steamer for Savannah, Georgia. He was not among the passengers saved but was drowned. His body was never recovered. Full description was sent to New Bedford and persons were sent to see if his body was recovered but it was never found. The last known of him as appears in the testimony was that he was in the state room with his two children and a waiter knocked on his door. He was never seen on deck and doubtless went*

down with the steamer. His father and mother were Frederick L Lapham
and Georgia A. Lapham of Savannah, Georgia.
February 25, 1884   Francis Wessuteen, Justice of the Peace

How this document surfaced is as intriguing as its provenance.[119]

The estate of Sampson Fawcett of Lawrence claimed that he booked steerage passage to Jacksonville, Florida, for fifteen dollars. The "night was clear and abundant moonlight." The ship "became broken and wrecked," and "no proper measures were taken by the officers and crew" to rescue passengers. Second Mate Harding "was not a pilot for the waters upon which the ship was then going." Negligence was widespread—no proper apparatus for launching boats, deficit construction of the bulkheads—and Sampson "suffered great mental and bodily pain and misery." All issues related to the claim "that there was negligence on the part of those employed by said Boston and Savannah Steamship Company."[120]

John Cook of Ferry Village, Maine, "after great suffering in the rigging for hours," jumped and was rescued, but he lost personal effects valued at $254.65. Cook detailed his losses: "one suit of clothes, $35; 1 pr undershirt and drawers, $3; 1 revolver and cartridge, $14.85; 1 necktie and pin, $5; and nine collars, $1.80."

James Kelly filed for Annie Kelly, who "fell, or was washed into the sea and drowned."

It was evident that the crew of the *City of Columbus* "showed a want of drill and proper regulations for such an emergency."

The company sought limited liability regarding the wreck, meaning it would not have to reimburse or pay out damages to passengers for their personal losses. The respondents' motion—that insurance monies be paid to the court—was denied. These issues were decided by the district court and appealed and affirmed by the circuit court.

The case was then appealed to the Supreme Court of the United States, which took up the issue of limited liability. The court responded to questions in the case.

First, did limited liability extend to all damages (i.e. personal injury and loss of life, as well as loss of or damage to property)? The court found it did; otherwise, limited liability serves no purpose.

Should the value of the ship and freight be insufficient to compensate all who sought damages, proceeds were to be divided in a pro rata manner, so each would receive a proportionate amount of the allocated funds. Libellants again denied any liability.

The value of the ship was deemed to be $2,100 after the disaster, as it lay on the ocean floor off Gay Head. That included the hull, machinery, tackle, apparel and furniture. Value of the cargo, which was to be delivered to Savannah, was $967.68. Prepaid passenger passage amounted to $963.55.

Exhibit A was the passenger list of eighty-three names, both stateroom and steerage, as well as baggage and personal effects. This list is no longer extant; at least, it was not included in the final report. Exhibit B detailed the cargo, which consisted of "boots, shoes, provisions, furniture and other merchandise."

The *City of Columbus* rested at anchor, with its canvas ventilator rigged. The ship was one of a fleet of popular steamships that plied the waters between Boston and Savannah, bearing both passengers and cargo, linking the North and the South. *Courtesy of Eric Takakjian/Quest Marine Services and the Mariner's Museum, Newport News, Virginia.*

Attorney George Dresser observes, "the dollar figure to which liability was limited was the value of the ship after the loss. That is, what is it worth lying there at the bottom of Vineyard Sound? Not much." Furthermore, he notes that "maybe the passengers' estates could at least get the insurance money. No such luck—that was payable to the mortgagees who had helped finance the purchase." And so the insurance monies went to outstanding notes due on the mortgage, and the only payout for the passengers or their estates was limited to the monies left over of the ship's value, which were minimal.

It was affirmed by the Supreme Court that limited liability applies in this case; thus, the decrees in both cases were affirmed. From initial claims of nearly $650,000, surviving passengers and estates of the deceased who had filed claims were awarded $3,885, to be split among them.

On May 2, 1889, the final decree was handed down "pursuant to the rules of the Supreme Court of the United States." The court issued a monition against all persons claiming damages for said loss, destruction, damage or injury. It was determined that the value of interest of the libellant was $3,885.83. Following is the list of recipients of the pro rata amount of funds distributed:

James Brown, $535.00
Samuel Fawcett, $267.50
James Walker, $267.50
Elizabeth Skene, $267.50
Frederick Milton Sargent, $267.50
Helon Brooks, $267.50
James Merrill, $267.50
Joel Nourse, $267.50
Elizabeth Beach, $267.50
B.E. Kelly, $267.50
Anna Kelly, $267.50
John Heaver, $267.50
John Cook, $66.09
Boston Marine Insurance, $305.11
George Roach, $26.06
GWH Litchfield, $1,107.00

And the final words the court issued were: "Upon such payment, the libellant shall be forever relieved, and discharged of, and from any and all claims, arising out of the loss, destruction, damage and injury done, occasioned or incurred by the stranding and sinking of said steamship as alleged in said libel."[121]

15
The Aftermath

The wreck quickly became part of local lore:

> Since the wreck of the City of Columbus *New Bedford children have been frequently noticed playing "wreck" as they call it. Recently, as several little ones were so engaged, using a box to represent the wreck, a little girl got into the box and held up her hands to be saved, whereupon a little boy shouted, Go back, go back; not a woman or child was saved.*[122]

In July, following the wreck, it was publicly noted that the *City of Columbus* was only one of many other vessels that had run aground in Vineyard Sound, recognized as a dangerous waterway. It was proposed that construction of a Cape Cod Ship Canal would eliminate this danger. The canal, however, was another thirty years in coming.[123]

Six months after the *City of Columbus* foundered on the Vineyard shores,[124] it was a destination for tourists curious about the perilous place where so many people perished. A newspaper report is jaunty: "'Oh, what a hot place' was probably the first thought entering the heads of 1,500 excursionists from Boston and way stations who landed yesterday at Gay Head, the scene of the ill-fated *City of Columbus* wreck."

The cliffs were the draw then as now: "As one approaches it on the steamboat the variegated colors and sharp outlines of the chalk cliffs [*sic*], looming up out of the water, present a beautiful and poetic sight." Transportation was limited: "The only method of conveyance from the pier to the observatory was by an ox cart." The wharf where the steamship docked was on the shoreline, just north of the lighthouse.

The ox cart was the primary means of transportation at Gay Head in the late nineteenth century. Tourists who visited the cliffs arrived by steamship and were transported in these conveyances. *Courtesy of the Martha's Vineyard Museum.*

The reporter noted:

> *There is no monument or memorial of any kind to commemorate the shipwreck, nor do any traces of it remain except in the broken fragments of wood the Indians peddle. The mast and part of the hull of the wreck, which were for a time visible, have now sunk under water. Divers are at work daily at the wreck, which has been bought by parties for the sake of the iron it contains.*

The tourists walked the shore near where the disaster occurred:

> *After inspecting the place, walking over the chalk cliffs, ascending the lighthouse and examining the medals which the humane society has presented to several of the Indians for their bravery at the time of the wreck, the excursionists were ready to return at 3:30. The sail back to New Bedford on the* Monahasset *was as pleasant as the sail down had been, except that 1,500 persons make a boat of that size overcrowded and*

dangerous. All were in good spirits, however, and enjoyed themselves hugely. Boston was reached at 8:20.

The reporter found no irony in the overloaded boat touring the scene of the terrible tragedy.

Another vantage of the wreck was taken from the perspective of a quarter century. Now the horror was evident in how people died: "It was a most appalling disaster, one of those sudden and unlooked for calamities, directly due to carelessness, which cause such shock and sorrow to those left bereaved."[125]

A cheerful throng departed on the *City of Columbus*:

> *There was a gay company on the steamship when she steamed out of Boston harbor, for most of the passengers were bound south to escape the rigors of*

This postcard of the Gay Head light and cliffs includes the Humane Society building in the distance. The lighthouse keeper's cottage was removed in the 1950s, when electricity reached Gay Head. The wreck occurred a half mile offshore from the lighthouse. *Courtesy of Judy and Peter Case.*

a New England winter, and the coldness of the day made them all the more joyful in the thought that they were leaving the frost king behind as fast as steam and the churning propeller could carry them.

The explanation of the tragedy was concise: "Thick weather or terrific storm was not responsible for the loss of the *City of Columbus*, as the death of so many of her passengers was directly due to the inattention of the second officer in charge of the pilot house at the time."

In 1939, George A. Hough Jr., publisher of the *Falmouth Enterprise*, ran a series of articles on the wreck: "Despite Captain Wright, it is accepted that the buoy was off to starboard. The *Columbus* had run well inside the marker, onto a reef hardly a quarter of a mile from one of the coast's most powerful lights." After this scathing assessment of deficient navigation, the *Enterprise* continued: "The fatal mistake was backing up into deeper water." Then, the ship upended, flooded and sank, taking more than one hundred people to their deaths.

Two days after the disaster, the *Enterprise* report continued, the *Nellie*, a tug filled with reporters and relatives, left New Bedford for Vineyard Haven. "They passed the wreck of the steamer and watched in silence as huge combers struck the bow of the death ship and foamed around the masts."

"What ifs" cloud our mind's eye:

Had the vessel been permitted to remain as she struck, all might possibly have been saved and the steamship salvaged later, but in the excitement the captain made the fatal blunder of ordering the engines reversed, and only too surely the powerful propeller pulled her from the edge, so that the sea rushed into the hole, and as she backed off she careened on her side.

The tragedy continued to unfold as "the volume of water rushing in carried the stairs away, leaving nearly 100 of the passengers trapped in the cabins to drown."

Excerpts from this extensive *Enterprise* report provided an impetus for George A. Hough Jr.'s well-researched *Disaster on Devil's Bridge* twenty-five years later.

Hanging from the shrouds was dangerous as well:

To add to the suffering of those who remained in the rigging, the wind freshened and the sea mounted higher and higher, the spray freezing on them as it struck.

A boat had been launched but had been crushed against the metal side of the steamship like an eggshell.

The captain of this valiant Indian crew, finding that heavy leather boots were filled with water, made them remove the boots to prevent their feet freezing, and in their stocking feet they made the second and successful effort to get their boat beyond the line of breakers.

The Indians of Gay Head were exceptionally kind to the survivors, and in addition to their brave work in rescuing the perishing, they worked long and untiringly in their efforts to collect the dead washed ashore or found floating in the sea.

Time has softened the blame that at the time was placed upon his [Wright's] shoulders, for he had been 20 hours without rest...but as a pilot, his duty had been to remain on deck until the steamship was clear of all land, although his chief blunder was in backing the vessel off the reef.

It was small consolation, in the years after the wreck, that other vessels foundered in the same area as the *City of Columbus*. In the summer of 1887, the *Gate City* and the *Panther* both ran ashore during dense fog at the same point as the *City of Columbus*. "In both these latter cases the captains allowed the steamship to stay on the reef where they struck, so that the people and even the cargoes were saved and later the vessels gotten off as well."[126]

A half century after the shipwreck, the *Globe* revisited it: "'Twas on a night like this, crisp and clear, just 53 years ago that a 'floating palace,' the *City of Columbus*, drove onto the jagged rocks of Devil's Bridge on Martha's Vineyard with a loss of 99 lives."[127] The reporter romanticized the atmosphere aboard ship on that fateful night:

In the ballroom of the big ship, passengers danced that night to the lilting tunes of the Eighties, and in the boat's hold grazed six cows contentedly as she headed South. As the boat's bell chimed midnight the passengers retired, the cows bedded down in their hay.

In an investigation that followed, tide and wind were blamed for driving the City of Columbus *from the channel onto the sunken shoals.*

And the *Boston Globe* reprised the wreck in verse in 1959, on the seventy-fifth anniversary of the tragedy:

THE WRECK OF THE CITY OF COLUMBUS[128]
by Billy Bell

There's the wreck of the fatal Columbus
On the Devil's Bridge Rocks, near Gay Head
Where the lives of one hundred poor people
Were lost in the wild waves, 'tis said.

Nearly all were asleep as the ship plowed the deep,
And the wind blew the waves mountain high.
With a terrible shock she was cast on a rock
And many were doomed there to die.

All the blame has been placed on young Harden [sic],
Who steered from his course toward the shore.
It was little those poor souls were dreaming
Such a sad fate for them was in store.

But I can't help condemning the captain
Of the Glaucus, *who swiftly sailed by,*
Leaving forty poor souls in the rigging
From exposure to suffer and die.

Epilogue

When 103 people died in the wreck of the *City of Columbus* in 1884, it was the worst loss of life in a shipwreck off the New England coast in the nineteenth century. Fourteen years later, in 1898, the *Portland* sank off Cape Ann, and 192 people died, in what became known as the Portland Gale. Twenty-eight years after the wreck of the *City of Columbus*, 1,517 people drowned when the "unsinkable" *Titanic* struck an iceberg and sank on April 15, 1912, on its maiden voyage. Many more wrecks have resulted in great loss of life, but few match the "cruelly causeless" wreck of the *City of Columbus*.

For more than a century, the *City of Columbus* has haunted Vineyarders. Whether it is antique artifacts in local households, stories passed down through families or questions raised about the cause of the wreck, the *City of Columbus* lives on. Generations have hungered for tangible evidence of the ship.

In the late 1950s, four teenagers set out to explore shipwrecks on Vineyard shores. They spent several seasons diving on the *Port Hunter* off East Chop. The lure of the *City of Columbus* drew them to Gay Head. Sam Low, Arnie Carr and the Jones brothers, Dick and Bill, patrolled the waters off Devil's Bridge in Sam Low's Chris-Craft.

In the creative genius of youth, Sam built an underwater sled to survey the ocean floor. Sam tells the tale: "I designed a sled. We'd seen something like it in the movies." It had a two-by-four frame with a plywood base. The boys towed the sled with a two-hundred-foot towline behind their boat. The innovation was that Sam attached fins to a curtain rod at the front of the sled. Lying on the sled, with air tanks, the teenage diver could steer the sled by moving his hands on the fins. "When you turn, you could sweep an area of twenty-five to thirty feet," Sam says. Visibility under water was about twelve to fifteen feet. "I was totally surprised how well this worked. Worked from day one." One cautionary note: the current off Gay Head is so strong that when you turn your head, you lose your mask. Day after day, they searched the waters for the elusive ship, but to no avail. Still, "the sled was great fun."

Arnie picks up the story. "In 1956, we scoured Gay Head, though we miscalculated in our search for the *City of Columbus*. We had a grid of Devil's Bridge, based on a photo of the *City of Columbus*. And we estimated the water depth of the bow and the stern." He explains another novel idea:

> *We used soda cans, half-filled with cement, painted bright colors and set out to search our grid. This is long before GPS or anything beyond a compass. Once we'd searched one area, we'd toss a can overboard to let us know where we'd been. One of us was towed on a sled, which was a lot of fun, until we thought we might be bait on a hook for some fish. By avoiding the massive underwater boulders that make up Devil's Bridge, we may have passed right over the wreck.*

Years passed. Sam Low worked with the National Geographic Society as an underwater archaeologist on Greek and Roman sites in the Mediterranean. He made films recording his adventures. Then he taught anthropology in college. Currently, he is completing a well-researched book on cultural and historical aspects of Hawaii.

Arnie Carr describes his passion: "I like doing wrecks, do the research, locate and identify." He worked for the state in the division of fisheries, as a marine biologist, for nearly forty years. He became proficient in the use of underwater cameras and submersibles. With his side-scan sonar, he can "read" items deep below the surface of the ocean. Arnie has earned an enviable reputation with his company, American Underwater Search and Survey.

Fast-forward forty years. A friendship formed in youth was rekindled when the opportunity arose to dive again. Arnie has a friend named Eric Takakjian (see chapter one). Eric discovered the wreck of the *City of Columbus* in the spring of 2000. As Arnie says, "Eric gave me the word. We both used the same photograph [taken the day after the wreck]. He popped right onto it. We trade information; we're friends." Because they are part of a tightknit community of divers, as well as friends, Eric shared the coordinates of the wreck.

"Arnie is a great guy," says Eric. "He and his partner, John Fish, are probably two of the best side scan guys in the world. They have accomplished many difficult shipwreck discoveries over the years, including finding the wreck of the steamship *Portland* off Cape Ann." The *Portland* was located in 2002.

In 2005, nearly a half century after their youthful diving exploits, Arnie reunited with his buddies, and they set out to find the *City of Columbus* for themselves.

"The chance came up to dive together again," recalls Sam. "*City of Columbus* was *the* wreck we wanted to find. It was the most elusive, and most famous, and it was a chance to dive together again."

With critical information about the location of the sunken vessel, Arnie brought his boat, the *Amphritite*, out to Devil's Bridge in the late summer of 2005, with his buddies on board. Sam refers to the *Amphritite* as "the perfect dive boat, well-equipped, with a cabin forward, pilot house and cockpit." This time, they were successful.

"We went over the site with the chart, making a series of parallel lines, watching the chart and the side-scan sonar," says Sam. "As I recall, we saw slight traces of the *City of Columbus* on our side-scan sonar." Arnie affirms the account. "We had no trouble finding the wreck. I brought my side-scan sonar so I could locate the wreck. No trouble."

Arnie recalls, "We dove again, together, and found the turn of the bilge [lower outer part of a ship's hull] but only about 20 percent of the edge of

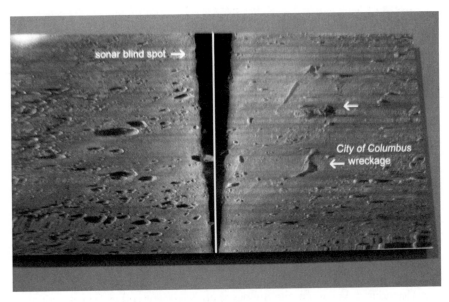

This side-scan sonar image of the wreck of the *City of Columbus* was taken by Rob Morris of *EdgeTech.com. Courtesy of the Martha's Vineyard Museum.*

the whole ship. There were slightly curved lines of the turn of the bilge. Part of the engine assembly sticks up with a little footprint. It's about fifteen feet." The wreck is almost buried in sand. Sam suggested the use of an air lift to suction sand up a tube, using an air compressor. This would free the ship for further exploration. Both men would love to dive again for the *City of Columbus*. Now that it has been located, the lure is even more enticing.

The magic and mystery of this shipwreck continue to intrigue and enthrall divers, maritime historians, curiosity-seekers and Vineyarders. Many levels of the disaster spur interest and involvement, from the horrors of the tragedy to the mystery of what really happened to allow a passenger steamer to run aground and so many people to die.

One shipwreck expert shares his opinion on the role the *City of Columbus* plays as a particular shipwreck among myriad wrecks in ocean waters. The thrill that drew Sam and Arnie back to the deep decades after their initial foray is evidenced by continued interest in learning more and sharing information about shipwrecks.

Jamin Wells writes:

> *I see the* City of Columbus *as representative of the thousands of shipwrecks along the American coast during the nineteenth century. As I see them, shipwrecks, disseminated through national media, were one of the primary ways in which most Americans first "experienced" the shore. From the lighthouse and* Dexter *intervention to the national media coverage, the* City of Columbus *was a wreck that brought the Vineyard, Aquinnah Wampanoag, and disaster into the conversations of Americans from Bangor to San Francisco. This is not to downplay the wreck's local significance— only to highlight that shipwrecks (like the* City of Columbus*) have a much broader (if more elusive) impact on local, regional, even national history.*

And so the story of the *City of Columbus* assumes an integral role in our past, with both local and national relevance. The people involved are long gone, but their medals and memories survive. The artifacts are mere symbols of the tragedy of the wreck; they leave us awed that a routine voyage rapidly turned into a disaster. That no women or children were saved is horrendous. Only 13 percent of the passengers survived, while 37 percent of the crew made it out alive. Blame was assigned, but lingering doubt hovers over the shipwreck; no one knows what Second Mate Gus Harding was doing or thinking in the moments before the vessel foundered. What remains are newspaper accounts, official documentation and the wonder at a shipwreck that never should have happened.

Notes

CHAPTER 1

1. The Board of Underwater Archaeological Resources, according to Director Victor Mastone, "does not restrict appropriate and responsible recreational access" but aims to "appropriately accommodate recreational use and encourage heritage tourism at these sites." That said, however, "there is insufficient information currently available" to include the wreck of the *City of Columbus* as such a site. Mr. Mastone notes that the location of the sunken vessel is known, "thus it may possess archaeological integrity. Given the heavy loss of life, it has strong memorial value and is a grave site (over 80 bodies were never recovered)." For more information visit www.mass.gov/czm/buar/index.htm.

CHAPTER 2

2. *Philadelphia Inquirer*, June 19, 1878 (reprinted in the *Columbus* [Georgia] *Daily Enquirer*, as well as the *New York Herald Tribune* and other papers).
3. Snow, *Storms and Shipwrecks*, 106.
4. *Boston Daily Advertiser*, January 21, 1884.
5. *Scientific American*, September 14, 1878.
6. Hough, *Disaster on Devil's Bridge*, 22.
7. *Boston Daily Advertiser*, September 14, 1882.

CHAPTER 3

8. *Boston Herald*, September 24, 1882.
9. Wilford White, the captain's son-in-law, assumed management and publication in 1910. His son, Robert E. White, and wife, Molly, printed the *Tide and Pilot Book* for many years. Today, fourth-generation Ridge White and his wife, Linda, publish *The Tide and Pilot Book*. The latest version offers personal observation, as well as government information; it is an indispensable nautical almanac, recognized on its cover as "the most trusted guide for East Coast waterways since 1875." For more information e-mail ebb2flood@gmail.com.

CHAPTER 4

10. *Maryland Sun*, September 18, 1883.
11. *Augusta* [Georgia] *Chronicle*, September 20, 1883.
12. Cahill, *New England Ghostly Haunts*.

CHAPTER 5

13. *Vineyard Gazette*, January 25, 1884.
14. *Providence Evening Press*, January 21, 1884.
15. *Providence Daily Journal*, January 19, 1884.
16. Ibid., January 26, 1884.
17. *Vineyard Gazette*, January 25, 1884.
18. *Providence Evening Press*, January 21, 1884.
19. Snow, *Storms and Shipwrecks*, 107.
20. *Yankee Magazine*, January 1958.
21. *Boston Journal*, January 21, 1884.
22. *Morning Mercury*, "Awful Tale," January 30, 1884.
23. *Vineyard Gazette*, January 25, 1884.
24. *Providence Evening Press*, January 21, 1884.
25. *Providence Daily Journal*, January 26, 1884. Articles in the *Providence Daily Journal* were transcribed by marine and shipwreck historian and diver Jim Jenney of Newport, Rhode Island. His interest extends "to shipwrecks throughout New England with a particular interest in steam vessels like the *City of Columbus*." Currently, he is researching and writing a historical account of shipwrecks in Rhode Island.

CHAPTER 6

26. Hough, *Disaster on Devil's Bridge*, 16.
27. Ibid. 15.
28. Ibid. 19.
29. Bill of fare aboard ship courtesy of Richard Boonisar, who has collected nautical artifacts for forty years.
30. *Weekly Mercury*, January 30, 1884.
31. *Vineyard Gazette*, January 25, 1884.
32. *Providence Daily Journal*, January 21, 1884.
33. *Frank Leslie's Illustrated News*, January 26, 1884.
34. A descendant of Hammond, T.S. Kent, contacted us. "My great-grandfather's brother was one of the passengers lost. If you go to my Hammond family tree you will see George Frederick Hammond, who died on the *Columbus*."
35. Ibid.; *Weekly Mercury*, January 30, 1884.

CHAPTER 7

36. *Weekly Mercury*, January 30, 1884.
37. *Vineyard Gazette*, January 25, 1884.
38. *Frank Leslie's Illustrated News*, February 2, 1884.
39. Scoville, *Shipwrecks on Martha's Vineyard*, 10.
40. *Frank Leslie's Illustrated News*, February 2, 1884.
41. Snow, *Storms and Shipwrecks*, 108.
42. *New York Times*, January 24, 1884.

CHAPTER 8

43. *Vineyard Gazette*, January 25, 1884.
44. Horatio Nelson Pease, the lighthouse keeper, was the son of Joseph Pease, founder of the Martha's Vineyard National Bank. Joseph also served as customs collector. In that capacity, he orchestrated the removal of the West Chop lighthouse back from the shore due to erosion. Horatio's grandfather, Jeremiah Pease, was the Methodist minister who founded Wesleyan Grove in Oak Bluffs. Horatio and his wife, Lydia Adams, had three children: Sophronia, Ada and Grace.

Pease was born in 1836 and died in 1919. Thanks to Rick Bart for this genealogical data.

45. *Vineyard Gazette*, February 15, 1884.

46. *Along the Coast* was a monthly magazine that chronicled efforts of the men of the U.S. Life Saving Service who manned lighthouses and lightships along the coast. They were known as surf men. Stories of shipwrecks and tales of the sea, as well as accounts of the lifesaving crews, filled the pages. Courtesy of James Claflin of Lighthouse Antiques.

47. Samuel Anthony was twenty-three at the time of the rescue and later married Maria Cook. They were great-grandparents of Beverly Wright, current Aquinnah selectperson. She has his medal in her possession.

48. *Providence Daily Journal,* January 22, 1884.

49. The homeport of the *Dexter* is unclear. Pease and Silva claim it was stationed in New London, and Scoville places it in New Bedford, while the Coast Guard states the ship was based out of Newport, Rhode Island.

50. *Harper's Weekly*, February 2, 1884.

51. *Vineyard Gazette*, February 1, 1884.

52. Pairpoint, *Rambles in America*, 29.

53. *New Bedford Morning Mercury*, December 7, 1898. "A telegram received in this city yesterday announced the shocking news of the death of Lieut. Charles D. Kennedy, formerly of this city, in an explosion in a powder factory at West Berkley, California."

54. Scoville, *Shipwrecks on Martha's Vineyard*, 9.

55. *Vineyard Gazette*, November 4, 1927.

56. Hough, *Disaster on Devil's Bridge*, 73.

CHAPTER 9

57. *Morning Mercury,* January 30, 1884.

58. *Evening Daily News,* January 22, 1884.

59. *Providence Daily Journal,* January 19, 1884.

60. *Cincinnati Tribune,* January 23, 1884.

61. *Vineyard Gazette,* January 25, 1884.

62. *Harper's Weekly,* February 2, 1884.

63. *Scientific American*, February 2, 1884, p. 68.

64. *Frank Leslie's Illustrated News*, February 2, 1884.

65. Ibid., January 26, 1884.

66. Pairpoint, *Rambles in America*, 18.
67. Ibid. 29.
68. Snow, *Storms and Shipwrecks.*
69. Hough, *Disaster on Devil's Bridge*, 106.
70. Scoville, *Shipwrecks on Martha's Vineyard*, 6.
71. Quinn, *Shipwrecks Around Cape Cod*, 69.
72. Farson, *12 Men Down*, 26.

Chapter 10

73. *Boston Journal*, January 25, 1884.
74. *Frank Leslie's Illustrated News*, February 2, 1884.
75. *Providence Daily Journal*, January 25, 1884.
76. Ron Crooker responded to a request on Ancestry.com and furnished this fascinating background on the circumstances of the Belyea family. "My daughter Kris visited the site at Gays Head [*sic*] a few years ago but found no-one who knew much of anything about the wreck. Anyway, that's a short summary of some of the circumstances surrounding the disastrous happenings to this Belyea family."
77. *New York Times*, January 28, 1884.
78. *Frank Leslie's Illustrated News*, February 2, 1884.
79. *New York Times*, January 23, 1884.
80. Farson, *12 Men Down*, 40.
81. *Fall River Evening Daily News*, January 22, 1884.
82. *Falmouth Enterprise*, July 14, 1939.
83. *New York Times*, January 24, 1884.
84. *Providence Daily Journal*, February 28, 1884.
85. Tale offered by Evan Smith. Smith's great-grandfather, William Gill, heard the story and recorded it.

Chapter 11

86. *Falmouth Enterprise*, July 14, 1939.
87. The steamer's bell was installed in the Lambert's Cove School, across from the church, according to longtime resident Mabelle Medowski.
88. *Frank Leslie's Illustrated News*, February 2, 1884.

89. *New York Times*, January 27, 1884.

90. *The Day* [New London, Connecticut], January 24, 1884. Courtesy of Jamin Wells.

91. *Morning Mercury*, January 23, 1884.

92. *New York Times*, January 29, 1884.

93. *Boston Daily Advertiser*, January 28, 1884.

94. *New Haven Evening Register*, April 1, 1884. Courtesy of Jamin Wells.

95. *New York Times*, February 4, 1884.

96. *New Haven Register*, February 25, 1884.

97. *New York Times*, February 13, 1884.

98. Ibid., February 12, 1884.

99. *Boston Journal*, August 9, 1884.

CHAPTER 12

100. *Vineyard Gazette*, February 1, 1884.

101. Ibid., February 8, 1884.

102. Howe, *Humane Society*.

103. *Vineyard Gazette*, February 22, 1884.

104. One aspect of the Hunt gun was that the projectile had 750 feet of line coiled inside, which played out when fired. The gun was designed by Edmund Hunt, of Weymouth; it was replaced by the Lyle gun, manufactured by David Lyle, and was used by the Coast Guard until 1952. The surf men of the Life Saving Service were proficient in use of this apparatus.

105. *Vineyard Gazette*, February 29, 1884.

106. The certificate, with elaborate calligraphy listing members of the crew, is in the collection of Richard Boonisar, who has researched artifacts on the U.S. Life Saving Service and the Humane Society. Mr. Boonisar owns the former Gurnet Point Life-Saving Station in Plymouth Harbor.

107. Representative Long had served as governor of Massachusetts and later became secretary of the navy under President McKinley.

108. *Harper's Weekly*, February 2, 1884.

109. The Humane Society of the Commonwealth of Massachusetts was formally incorporated in 1786.

Chapter 13

110. *New York Times*, January 20, 1884.
111. We were unable to obtain a copy of the report of the inspectors, even with a trip to the National Archives in Waltham, Massachusetts. However, with the aid of the *Boston Journal*, the *Morning Mercury* of New Bedford and the *Providence Daily Journal*, we pieced together the investigation conducted by the steamship inspectors.
112. *Vineyard Gazette*, February 8, 1884.
113. *Boston Journal*, January 22, 1884.

Chapter 14

114. *Providence Daily Journal*, February 19, 1884.
115. Ibid.
116. Final Report, National Archives, Waltham, Massachusetts.
117. Ibid., 701.
118. Hough, *Disaster on Devil's Bridge*, 98.
119. It is fascinating how this affidavit came into the possession of Cheryl Sloane. She writes, "The letter actually came into my mother's possession after her mother (my grandmother) passed away. We have no relation to the deceased. We are not exactly sure how my grandmother came to have this letter. However, my mother does have a memory of my grandmother telling her that she found some old 'legal' type papers in their back yard in the days following the Worcester Tornado of 1953. My mother was a teenager at the time and did not pay much attention to my grandmother's finding. It was not until after my grandmother's death that my mother happened to come upon a box of old papers including the letter attached. This is when she surmised that these letters were the letters my grandmother had found in her yard back in 1953. This in itself is interesting as they lived about 60 miles East/Southeast of Worcester. In the years following my grandmother's death, my mother and I became curious about the sinking of the ship *Columbus* and that's when I first put my posting on the ancestry.com message board."
120. Final Report, 691.
121. Ibid., 827.

CHAPTER 15

122. *Worcester Daily Spy*, February 20, 1884.
123. *Committee of the Whole House on the State of the Union*, Serial Set Vol. 2259, Report on H. Rpt. 2040.
124. *Boston Daily Globe* August 16, 1884.
125. Ibid., January 15, 1911.
126. Ibid., January 20, 1937.
127. Ibid.
128. Ibid., July 5, 1959. Poem read by Mrs. L.H. of Melrose, Massachusetts/ Key West, Florida.